Stefan Zweig
SHOOTING STARS

Stefan Zweig
SHOOTING STARS
Ten Historical Miniatures

*Translated from the
German by Anthea Bell*

**PUSHKIN
PRESS**

Pushkin Press
71–75 Shelton Street,
London WC2H 9JQ

Original text © Williams Verlag AG Zurich
English translation © Anthea Bell, 2013

'The Field of Waterloo', 'The Discovery of El Dorado'
and 'The Race to Reach the South Pole' published
in German in *Sternstunden der Menschheit*, 1927.

'Flight into Immortality', 'The Conquest of Byzantium', 'The
Resurrection of George Frideric Handel', 'The Genius of a Night',
'The First Word to Cross the Ocean' and 'The Sealed Train' first
published in German in *Sternstunden der Menschheit*, 1940 edition.

'Wilson's Failure' first published in English (translated by Eden
and Cedar Paul) in 1940, in *The Tide of Fortune: Twelve Historical
Miniatures*, and added to later German editions.

This translation first published by Pushkin Press in 2013

ISBN 978 1782270 15 7

All rights reserved. No part of this publication may be reproduced,
stored in a retrieval system or transmitted in any form or by
any means, electronic, mechanical, photocopying, recording or
otherwise, without prior permission in writing from Pushkin Press

Set in 10 on 13 Monotype Baskerville
by Tetragon, London

Proudly printed and bound in Great Britain by TJ International,
Padstow, Cornwall on Munken Premium Cream 80gsm

www.pushkinpress.com

CONTENTS

Foreword	7
Flight into Immortality	9
The Conquest of Byzantium	39
The Resurrection of George Frideric Handel	73
The Genius of a Night	101
The Field of Waterloo	125
The Discovery of El Dorado	145
The First Word to Cross the Ocean	159
The Race to Reach the South Pole	187
The Sealed Train	211
Wilson's Failure	227

FOREWORD

No artist is an artist through the entire twenty-four hours of his normal day; he succeeds in producing all that is essential, all that will last, only in a few, rare moments of inspiration. History itself, which we may admire as the greatest writer and actor of all time, is by no means always creative. Even in "God's mysterious workshop", as Goethe reverently calls historical knowledge, a great many indifferent and ordinary incidents happen. As everywhere in life and art, sublime moments that will never be forgotten are few and far between. As a chronicler, history generally does no more than arrange events link by link, indifferently and persistently, fact by fact in a gigantic chain reaching through the millennia, for all tension needs a time of preparation, every incident with any true significance has to develop. Millions of people in a nation are necessary for a single genius to arise, millions of tedious hours must pass before a truly historic shooting star of humanity appears in the sky.

But if artistic geniuses do arise, they will outlast their own time; if such a significant hour in the history of the world occurs, it will decide matters for decades and centuries yet to come. As the electricity of the entire atmosphere is discharged at the tip of a lightning conductor, an immeasurable wealth of events is then crammed together in a small span of time. What usually happens at a leisurely pace, in sequence and due order, is concentrated into a single moment that determines and establishes everything: a single *Yes*, a single *No*, a *Too Soon* or a *Too Late* makes that hour irrevocable for hundreds of generations while deciding the life of a single man or woman, of a nation, even the destiny of all humanity.

Such dramatically compressed and fateful hours, in which a decision outlasting time is made on a single day, in a single hour, often just in a minute, are rare in the life of an individual and rare in the course of history. In this book I am aiming to remember the hours of such shooting stars—I call them that because they outshine the past as brilliantly and steadfastly as stars outshine the night. They come from very different periods of time and very different parts of the world. In none of them have I tried to give a new colour or to intensify the intellectual truth of inner or outer events by means of my own invention. For in those sublime moments when they emerge, fully formed, history needs no helping hand. Where the muse of history is truly a poet and a dramatist, no mortal writer may try to outdo her.

FLIGHT INTO IMMORTALITY

THE DISCOVERY OF THE PACIFIC OCEAN

---

25 September 1513

A SHIP IS FITTED OUT

When he first returned from the newly discovered continent of America, Columbus had displayed countless treasures and curiosities on his triumphal procession through the crowded streets of Seville and Barcelona: human beings of a race hitherto unknown, with reddish skins; animals never seen before; colourful, screeching parrots; slow-moving tapirs; then strange plants and fruits that would soon find a new home in Europe—Indian corn, tobacco, the coconut. The rejoicing throng marvels at all these things, but the royal couple and their counsellors are excited above all by a few boxes and baskets containing gold. Columbus does not bring much gold back from the new Indies: a few pretty things that he has bartered with the natives, or stolen from them, a few small bars and several handfuls of loose grains, gold dust rather than solid gold—the whole of it at most enough to mint a few hundred ducats. But the inspired Columbus, who always fanatically believes whatever he wants to believe at any given time, and who has been so gloriously proved right about his sea route to India, boasts effusively and in all honesty that this is only a tiny foretaste. Reliable news, he adds, has reached him of gold mines of immeasurable extent on these new islands; only just below the surface, the precious metal, he says, lies under a thin layer of soil in many fields, and you can easily dig it out with an ordinary spade. Farther south, however, there are realms where the kings drink from golden goblets, and gold is worth less than lead at home in Spain. The ever-avaricious king listens, intoxicated to hear of this new Ophir that now belongs to him. No one yet knows Columbus and his sublime folly well enough to doubt his promises. A great fleet is fitted out at once for the second voyage, and now there is no need for recruiting officers and drummers to find men to join it. Word of the newly discovered Ophir, where you can pick up gold from the ground with your bare hands, sends all Spain mad; people come in their hundreds, their thousands to travel to El Dorado, the land of gold.

But what a dismal tidal wave of humanity is now cast up by greed from every city, every village, every hamlet. Not only do honourable noblemen arrive, wishing to gild their coats of arms, not only are there bold adventurers and brave soldiers; all the filthy scum of Spain is also washed up in Palos and Cádiz. There are branded thieves, highwaymen and footpads hoping to find a more profitable trade in the land of gold; there are debtors who want to escape their creditors and husbands hoping to get away from scolding wives; all the desperadoes and failures, branded criminals and men sought by the Alguacil justices volunteer for the fleet, a motley band of failures who are determined that they will make their fortunes at long last, in an instant too, and to that end are ready to commit any act of violence and any crime. They have told one another the fantasies of Columbus, repeating that in those lands you have only to thrust a spade into the ground to see nuggets of gold glinting up at you, and the prosperous among the emigrants hire servants and mules to carry large quantities of the precious metal away. Those who do not succeed in being taken on by the expedition find another way: never troubling to get the royal permission, coarse-grained adventurers fit out ships for themselves, in order to cross the ocean as fast as they can and get their hands on gold, gold, gold. And at a single stroke, Spain is rid of troublemakers and the most dangerous kind of rabble.

The Governor of Española (later San Domingo and Haiti) is horrified to see these uninvited guests overrunning the island entrusted to his care. Year after year the ships bring new freight and increasingly rough, unruly fellows. The newcomers, in turn, are bitterly disappointed. There is no sign of gold lying loose on the road, and not another grain of corn can be got out of the unfortunate native inhabitants on whom these brutes descend. So hordes of them wander around, intent on robbery, terrifying the unhappy Indios and the governor alike. The latter tries in vain to make them colonists by showing them where land may be had, giving them cattle, and indeed ample supplies of human cattle in the form of sixty to seventy native inhabitants as slaves to work for every one of them. But neither the high-born hidalgos nor the former footpads have a mind to set up as farmers. They didn't come here to grow wheat and herd cattle; instead of putting their minds to sowing seed and harvesting crops, they torment the unfortunate Indios—they will have eradicated the entire indigenous population within a few years—or sit around in taverns. Within a short time most of them are so deep in debt that after their goods they have to sell their hats and coats, their last shirts, and they fall into the clutches of traders and usurers.

So in 1510 all these failures on Española are glad to hear that a well-regarded man from the island, the *bachiller* or lawyer Martín Fernandez de Enciso, is fitting out a ship with a new crew to come to the aid of his colony on terra firma. In 1509 two famous adventurers, Alonzo de Ojeda and Diego de Nicuesa, received the privilege from King Ferdinand of founding a colony near the straits of Panama and the coast of Venezuela, naming it rather too hastily Castilla del Oro, Golden Castile. Intoxicated by the resonant name and beguiled by tall stories, the lawyer, who knew little about the ways of the world, had put most of his fortune into this adventure. But now no gold comes from the newly founded colony in San Sebastián on the Gulf of Urabá, only shrill cries for help. Half the crew have been killed in fighting the native people, and the other half have starved to death. To save the investment he has already made, Enciso ventures the rest of his fortune, and equips another expedition to go to the aid of the original one. As soon as they hear that Enciso needs soldiers, all the desperadoes and loafers on Española exploit this opportunity and take ship with him. Their aim is simply to get away, away from their creditors and the watchful eyes of the stern governor. But the creditors are also on their guard. They realize that the worst of their debtors intend to disappear, never to be seen again, and so they besiege the governor with requests to let no one travel without his special permission. The governor grants their wish. A strict guard obliges Enciso's ship to stay outside the harbour, while government boats patrol the coastal waters to prevent anyone without such permission from being smuggled aboard. And all the embittered desperadoes, who fear death less than honest work or their towering debts, watch as Enciso's ship leaves on its venture with all sail set.

THE MAN IN THE CRATE

And so, with all sail set, Enciso's ship leaves Española and steers towards the American mainland. The outlines of the island it has left behind are already merging with the blue horizon. It is a calm voyage, and there is nothing in particular to be said about its early stages, or at most we may note that a huge and extremely powerful bloodhound—a son of the famous Becericco, who has become famous himself under the name of Leoncico—prowls restlessly up and down the deck, sniffing around everywhere. No one knows who owns the mighty animal or how he came on board. Finally the crew notice that the dog cannot be prised away from a particularly large crate of provisions that was brought aboard at the last minute. But lo and behold, this crate unexpectedly opens of its own accord, and out climbs a man of about thirty-five, well armed with sword, helmet and shield like Santiago, the patron saint of Castile. He is Vasco Núñez de Balboa, giving us the first evidence of his astonishing boldness and resource. Born in Jerez de los Caballeros of a noble family, he had sailed for the New World with Rodrigo de Bastidas as a private soldier and finally, after many wanderings, was stranded off Española along with his ship. The governor had tried in vain to make Núñez de Balboa into a good colonist; after a few months he had abandoned his allotted parcel of land and was bankrupt, and at a loss for a way to escape his creditors. But while the other debtors, clenching their fists, stare from the beach at the government boats that prevent them from getting away on Enciso's ship, Núñez de Balboa circumvents Diego Columbus's cordon by hiding in an empty provisions crate and getting accomplices to carry him aboard, where no one notices his cunning trick in all the tumult of putting out to sea. Only when he knows the ship is so far from the coast that the crew are unlikely to sail back to Española on his account does the stowaway emerge, and now here he is.

The *bachiller* Enciso is a man of law, and like lawyers in general has little romanticism in his soul. As Alcalde, chief of police in the new colony, he does not intend to put up with dubious characters. He brusquely informs Núñez de Balboa that he is not going to have him on his ship, but will put him ashore on the beach of the next island they pass, whether or not it is inhabited.

However, it never comes to that. For even as the ship is making for Castilla del Oro it meets—miraculously, in a time when only a few dozen vessels in all sail these still-unfamiliar seas—a heavily manned boat under a commander whose name will soon echo through the world, Francisco Pizarro. The men in the boat are from Enciso's colony of San Sebastián, and at first they are taken for mutineers who have left their posts of their own accord. But to Enciso's horror, they tell him there is no San Sebastián left, they themselves are the former colonists, their commander Ojeda has made off with one ship, the rest, who had only two brigantines, had to wait until all but seventy colonists had died before they could find room for themselves in the two small boats. One of those brigantines has been wrecked in its own turn; Pizarro's thirty-five men are the last survivors of Castilla del Oro. So now where are they to go? After hearing Pizarro's tale, Enciso's men have no taste for braving the swamp-like climate and the natives' poison-tipped arrows in the abandoned settlement; turning back to Española seems to them the only option. At this dangerous moment, Vasco Núñez de Balboa suddenly steps forward. He explains that after going on his first voyage with Rodrigo de Bastidas, he knows the whole coast of Central America, and he remembers that at the time of that voyage they found a place called Darién on the bank of a gold-bearing river where the natives were friendly. They should found the new settlement there, he suggests, not in this unhappy place.

At once the whole crew comes down on Núñez de Balboa's side. In line with his proposition, they steer for Darién on the Panama isthmus, where they first indulge in the usual slaughter of the natives, and as some gold is found among the goods they rob, the desperadoes decide to found a settlement here, in pious gratitude naming the new town Santa María de la Antigua del Darién.

A DANGEROUS RISE

The unfortunate financier of the colony, the *bachiller* Enciso, will soon be sorry he did not throw the crate overboard with Núñez de Balboa inside it, for after a few weeks that audacious man has all the power in his hands. As a lawyer who grew up believing in order and discipline, Enciso tries to administer the colony on behalf of the Spanish Crown in his capacity as Alcalde, the chief of police of the governor, who cannot be found just now, and enacts his edicts as sternly in the wretched huts of the Indios as if he were sitting in his legal chambers in Seville. In the middle of this wilderness where no humans have ever trod before, he forbids the soldiers to haggle over gold with the natives, gold being reserved for the Crown; he tries to force this undisciplined rabble to observe law and order, but the adventurers instinctively back a man of the sword rather than a man of the pen. Soon Balboa is the real master of the colony; Enciso has to flee to save his life, and when Nicuesa, one of the governors appointed to the mainland by the king, finally arrives to enforce the law Balboa refuses to let him land. The unhappy Nicuesa, hunted out of the land allotted to him by the king, drowns on the voyage back.

So now Núñez de Balboa, the man from the crate, lords it over the colony. But in spite of his success he does not feel very comfortable about it. He has openly rebelled against the king, and can hardly hope for pardon because it is his fault that the appointed governor is dead. He knows that Enciso, who has fled, is on his way to Spain with his complaints, and sooner or later he, Balboa, will be brought to trial for his rebellion. All the same, Spain is far away, and he has plenty of time left, all the time it takes for a ship to cross the ocean twice. Being as clever as he is bold, he looks for the only way to hold the power he has usurped for as long as possible. He knows that at this time success justifies all crimes, and a large delivery of gold to the royal treasury may well moderate or delay any punishment. So first he must lay hands on gold, for gold is power! Together with Francisco Pizarro, he subjugates and robs the indigenous people of the vicinity, and in the midst of the usual slaughter he achieves a crucial success. One of the natives, Careta by name, suggests that as he is already likely to die he might prefer not to make enemies of the Indios, and instead conclude an alliance with Careta's own tribe, offering him his daughter's hand as a pledge of his own good faith. Núñez de Balboa immediately recognizes the importance of having a reliable and powerful friend among the natives; he accepts Careta's offer, and—what is even more surprising—he remains an affectionate lover of the Indian girl until his last hour. Together with Careta he defeats all the local Indios, and acquires such authority among them that in the end the mightiest of their chieftains, Comagre by name, respectfully invites him to his home.

This visit to the powerful Indio chief ushers in a decision of great importance to international history as well as to the life of Vasco Núñez de Balboa, who has hitherto been only a desperado and bold rebel against the Crown of Spain, destined by the law courts of Castile to die by the axe or the noose. Comagre receives him in a stone house with spacious rooms, a dwelling that astonishes Vasco Núñez by the wealth of its furnishings; and, unasked, the chieftain makes his guest a present of 4,000 ounces of gold. And now it is Comagre's turn to be astonished, for as soon as the Sons of Heaven, the mighty and godlike strangers whom he has received with such reverence, set eyes on the gold there is an end to their dignity. Like dogs let off the chain they attack one another, swords are drawn, fists clenched, they shout and rage, every man wants his own share of the gold. The Indio chief watches the disorder in scornful surprise; his is the eternal amazement of children of nature the world over at those cultured people to whom a handful of yellow metal appears more precious than all the intellectual and technical achievements of their civilization.

At last the native chief addresses them, and with a shiver of greed the Spaniards hear what the interpreter translates. How strange, says Comagre, that you quarrel with each other over such small things, that you expose your lives to the utmost discomfort and danger for the sake of such a common metal. Over there, beyond those mountains, lies a huge lake, and all the rivers that flow into it bring gold down with them. A people live there who have ships like yours, with sails and oars, and their kings eat and drink from golden vessels. You can find as much of this yellow metal there as you want. It is a dangerous journey, for the chieftains on the way will certainly refuse to let you pass, but it would take only a few days.

Vasco Núñez de Balboa feels his heart contract. At last he is on the track of the legendary land of gold, the land that they have dreamt of for years and years; his predecessors have hoped for a sight of it in the south and the north, and now, if this native is telling the truth, it lies only a few days' journey away. And at the same time he had proof of the existence of that other ocean to which Columbus, Cabot, Corte-Real, all those great and famous seafarers, have sought the way in vain, and the way around the globe is discovered too. The name of the man who is first to see that new sea and take possession of it for his motherland will never perish on this earth. Now Balboa knows what he must do to absolve himself of all blame and win everlasting honour: he must be first to cross the isthmus to the Mar del Sur, the southern sea that is the way to India, and conquer this new Ophir for the Spanish Crown. That hour in the chief Comagre's house has determined his fate. From now on, the life of this chance-come adventurer has a higher meaning, one that will outlast time.

FLIGHT INTO IMMORTALITY

There can be no greater happiness in the life of a man than to have discovered his life's purpose in the middle of its span, in his years of creativity. Núñez de Balboa knows what is at stake for him—either a pitiful death on the scaffold or immortality. First he must buy peace with the Crown, in retrospect legitimizing and legalizing his crime when he usurped power! So the rebel of yesterday, now the most zealous of subjects, sends Pasamonte, the royal treasurer on Española, not only the one-fifth of Comagre's gift of gold that belongs to the Crown by law, but as he is better versed in the practices of the world than that dry lawyer Enciso he adds to the official consignment a private financial donation to the treasurer, asking to be confirmed in his office as Captain-General of the colony. In fact Pasamonte the treasurer has no authority to do so, but in return for the gold he sends Núñez de Balboa a provisional, if in truth worthless, document. At the same time Balboa, wishing to secure himself on all sides, has also sent two of his most reliable men to Spain to tell the court about all he has done for the Crown, conveying the important information that he has induced the Indio chieftain to support him. He needs, Vasco Núñez de Balboa tells the authorities in Seville, only a troop of 1,000 men, and with those men he will undertake to do more for Castile than any other Spaniard before him. He engages to discover the new sea and gain possession of the Land of Gold, now located at long last, the land promised by Columbus that never materialized but that he, Balboa, will conquer.

Everything now seems to have turned out well for the man who was once a rebel and a desperado. But the next ship from Spain brings bad news. One of his accomplices, a man whom he sent over to defuse the complaints at court of the robbed Enciso, tells him that such a mission is dangerous for him, even mortally dangerous. The cheated *bachiller* has gone to the Spanish law courts with his accusation of the man who robbed him of his power, and Balboa must pay him compensation. Meanwhile, the news of the nearby southern sea, which might have saved him, has not arrived yet; in any case, the next ship to cross the ocean will bring a lawyer to call Balboa to account for the trouble he has caused, and either judge him on the spot or take him back to Spain in chains.

Vasco Núñez de Balboa realizes that he is lost. He has been condemned before his message about the nearby southern sea and the Golden Coast arrives. Naturally news of it will be exploited even as his head rolls into the sand—someone else will bring his deed to completion, the great deed that he dreamt of. He himself can hope for nothing more from Spain. They know there that he hounded the king's rightful governor to his death, that he personally drove the Alcalde out of office—he will have to consider the verdict merciful if it is merely imprisonment, and he does not have to pay for his deeds on the block. He cannot count on powerful friends, for he has no power of his own left, and his best advocate, the gold, has too soft a voice to ensure mercy for him. Only one thing can save him now from the punishment for his audacity, and that is even greater audacity. If he discovers the other sea and the new Ophir before the lawyers arrive, and their henchmen take him and put him in fetters, he can save himself. Only one kind of flight is open to him here at the end of the inhabited world: flight into a great achievement, into immortality.

So Núñez de Balboa decides not to wait for the 1,000 men he asked Spain to send for the conquest of the unknown ocean, still less for the arrival of the lawyers. Better to venture on a monstrous deed with a few like-minded men! Better to die honourably for one of the boldest ventures of all times than be dragged shamefully to the scaffold with his hands bound. Núñez de Balboa calls the colony together, explains, without concealing the difficulties, his intention of crossing the isthmus, and asks who will follow him. His courage puts fresh heart into the others. A hundred and ninety soldiers, almost the entire defensive force of the colony capable of bearing arms, volunteer. There is not much equipment to be found, for these men are already living in a state of constant warfare. And on 1st September 1513 Núñez de Balboa, hero and bandit, adventurer and rebel, intent on escaping the gallows or a dungeon, sets out on his march into immortality.

AN IMMORTAL MOMENT

They begin to cross the isthmus in the province of Coyba, the little realm of the chief Careta whose daughter is Balboa's companion; it will later turn out that Núñez de Balboa has not chosen the narrowest place, in his ignorance thus extending the dangerous crossing by several days. But for such a bold venture into the unknown, his main concern is to have the security of a friendly Indian tribe, for support or in the case of a withdrawal. His men cross from Darién to Coyba in ten large canoes, 190 soldiers armed with spears, swords, arquebuses and crossbows, accompanied by a pack of the much-feared bloodhounds. His ally the Indian chief provides Indios to act as guides and bearers, and on 6th September the famous march across the isthmus begins, a venture making enormous demands on the will-power of those tried and tested adventurers. The Spanish first have to cross the low-lying areas in stifling equatorial heat that saps their strength; the marshy ground, full of feverish infections, was to kill many thousands of men working on the building of the Panama Canal centuries later. From the first they have to hack their way through the untrodden, poisonous jungle of creepers with axes and swords. The first of the troop, as if working inside a huge green mine, cut a narrow tunnel through the undergrowth for the others, and the army of conquistadors then strides along in single file, an endlessly long line of men, always with weapons in their hands, on the alert both day and night to repel any sudden attack by the native Indios. The heat is stifling in the sultry, misty darkness of the moist vault of giant trees as a pitiless sun blazes down above them. Drenched in sweat and with parched lips, the heavily armed men drag themselves on, mile after mile. Sometimes sudden downpours of rain fall like a hurricane, little streams instantly become torrential rivers, and the men have to either wade through them or cross them over swaying bridges improvised from palm fibres by the Indios. The Spanish have nothing to eat but a handful of maize; weary with lack of sleep, hungry, thirsty, surrounded by myriads of stinging, blood-sucking insects, they work their way forward in garments torn by thorns, footsore, their eyes feverish, their cheeks swollen by the stings of the whirring midges, restless by day, sleepless by night, and soon they are entirely exhausted. Even after the first week of marching, a large part of the troop can no longer stand up to the stress, and Núñez de Balboa, who knows that the real danger still lies in wait for them, gives orders for all those sick with fever and worn out to stay behind. He means to brave the crucial venture only with the best of his troop.

At last the ground begins to rise. The jungle becomes less dense now that its full tropical luxuriance can unfold only in the marshy hollows. But when there is no shade to protect them, the equatorial sun high overhead, glaring and hot, beats down on their heavy armour. Slowly and by short stages, the weary men manage to climb the hilly country to the mountain chain that separates the narrow stretch of land between the two oceans like a stone backbone. Gradually the view is freer, and the air is refreshing by night. After eighteen days of heroic effort, they seem to have overcome the worst difficulty; already the crest of the mountain range rises before them, and from the peaks, so the Indian guides say, they will be able to see both oceans, the Atlantic and the still-unknown and unnamed Pacific. But now of all times, just when they seem to have overcome the tough, vicious resistance of nature, they face a new enemy: the native chieftain of that province, who bars the strangers' way with hundreds of his warriors. Núñez de Balboa has plenty of experience of fighting off the Indios. All he has to do is get the men to fire a salvo from their arquebuses, and that artificial thunder and lightning exerts its proven magical power once again over the local population. Screaming, the terrified warriors run, the Spanish and their bloodhounds in pursuit. Instead of enjoying this easy victory, however, Balboa, like all the Spanish conquistadors, dishonours it by terrible cruelty, having a number of defenceless, bound prisoners torn apart alive by the hungry dogs, their flesh reduced to scraps, a spectacle staged as a substitute for bullfights and gladiatorial games. Dreadful slaughter shames the last night before Núñez de Balboa's immortal day.

There is a unique, inexplicable mixture in the character and manner of these Spanish conquistadors. Pious believers as ever any Christians were, they call upon God from the ardent depths of their souls, at the same time committing the most shocking inhumanities of history in his name. Capable of the most magnificent and heroic feats of courage, sacrifice and suffering, they still deceive and fight one another shamelessly; yet in the midst of their contemptible behaviour they have a strong feeling of honour, and a wonderful, indeed truly admirable sense of the historic importance of their mission. That same Núñez de Balboa who threw innocent, bound and defenceless prisoners to the bloodthirsty dogs the evening before, perhaps caressing the jaws of the animals in satisfaction while they were still dripping with human blood, understands the precise significance of his deed in the story of mankind, and at the crucial moment finds one of those great gestures that remain unforgettable over the ages. He knows that this day, the 25th of September, will be remembered in the history of the world, and with true Spanish feeling the hard, thoughtless adventurer lets it be known how fully he has grasped the lasting gravity of his mission.

Balboa's gesture is this: that evening, directly after the bloodbath, one of the natives has pointed out a nearby peak, telling him that from its height you can see the other ocean, the unknown Mar del Sur. Immediately Balboa makes his arrangements. Leaving the injured and exhausted men in the plundered village, he orders those still capable of marching—sixty-seven of them in all, out of the original 190 with whom he began the expedition in Darién—to climb the mountain. They approach the peak at ten in the morning. There is only a small, bare hilltop yet to be scaled, and then the view must stretch out before their eyes.

At this moment Balboa commands his men to stop. None of them is to follow him, for he does not want to share this first sight of the new ocean with anyone else. After crossing one gigantic ocean in our world, the Atlantic, he alone will be, now and for ever, the first Spaniard, the first European, the first Christian to set eyes on the still-unknown other ocean, the Pacific. Slowly, with his heart thudding, deeply aware of the significance of the moment, he climbs on, a flag in his left hand, his sword in his right hand, a solitary silhouette in the vast orb. Slowly he scales the hilltop, without haste, for the real work has already been done. Only a few more steps, fewer now, still fewer, and once he has reached the peak a great view opens up before him. Beyond the mountains, wooded and green as the hills descend below him, lies an endless expanse of water with reflections as of metal in it: the sea, the new and unknown sea, hitherto only dreamt of and never seen, the legendary sea sought in vain by Columbus and all who came after him, the ocean whose waves lap against the shores of America, India and China. And Vasco Núñez de Balboa looks and looks and looks, blissfully proud as he drinks in the knowledge that his are the first European eyes in which the endless blue of that ocean is mirrored.

Vasco Núñez de Balboa gazes long and ecstatically into the distance. Only then does he call up his comrades to share his joy and pride. Restless and excited, gasping for breath and crying out aloud, they scramble, climb and run up the last hill, they stare in amazement and gaze with astonishment in their eyes. All of a sudden Father Anselm de Vara, who is with the party, strikes up the *Te Deum laudamus*, and at once all the noise and shouting dies down, all the harsh, rough voices of those soldiers, adventurers and bandits uniting in the devout hymn. The Indios watch in astonishment as, at a word from the priest, they cut down a tree to erect a cross, carving the initials of the King of Spain's name in the wood. And when the cross rises, it is as if its two wooden arms were reaching out to both seas, the Atlantic and the Pacific Oceans, and all the hidden distance beyond them.

In the midst of the awed silence, Núñez de Balboa steps forward and addresses his soldiers. They did right, he says, to thank God who of his grace has granted them such honour, and pray to him to continue helping them to conquer that sea and all these lands. If they will continue following him faithfully, he adds, they will go home from these new Indies the richest Spaniards ever known. He solemnly raises his flag to all four winds, to take possession on behalf of Spain of all the distant lands where those winds blow. Then he calls the clerk, Andrés de Valderrabáno, telling him to write out a certificate recording this solemn act for all time to come. Andrés de Valderrabáno unrolls a parchment that he has carried in a closed wooden container with an inkwell and a quill all the way through the jungle, and commands all the noblemen and knights and men-at-arms—*los caballeros e hidalgos y hombres de bien*—"who were present at the discovery of the southern sea, the Mar del Sur, by the noble and highly honoured Captain Vasco Núñez de Balboa, His Majesty's Governor", to confirm that "this Master Vasco Núñez de Balboa was the man who first set eyes on that sea and showed it to his followers".

Then the sixty-seven men climbed down the hill, and since that day, the 25th of September 1513, mankind has known of the last and hitherto undiscovered ocean on earth.

GOLD AND PEARLS

At last they are certain of it. They have seen the sea. And now to go down to its coast, feel the flowing water, touch it, taste it, pick up flotsam and jetsam from the beach! It takes them two days to climb down, and so that in future he will know the quickest way from the mountain range to the sea, Núñez de Balboa divides his men into separate groups. The third of these groups, under Alonzo Martín, is the first to arrive on the beach, and even the simple soldiers of this group of adventurers are so full of the vanity of fame, so thirsty for immortality, that Alonzo Martín himself, a plain, straightforward man, instantly gets the clerk to write down in black and white that he was the first to plunge his foot and his hand in those still-unnamed waters. Only after he has exchanged his small ego for a mote of immortality does he let Balboa know that he has reached the sea and felt its water with his own hand. Balboa immediately prepares for another grand gesture. Next day, Michaelmas Day by the calendar, he appears with only twenty-two companions on the beach, armed and girded like St Michael himself, to take possession of the new sea in a solemn ceremony. He does not stride into the water at once, but waits haughtily like its lord and master, resting under a tree until the rising tide sends a wave washing up to him, licking around his feet like an obedient dog. Only then does he stand up, slinging his shield on his back so that it gleams like a mirror in the sun, take his sword in one hand and in the other the flag of Castile bearing the portrait of the Virgin Mary, and stride into the water. Not until he is deep in those vast, strange waters, the waves breaking round his waist, does Núñez de Balboa, once a rebel and desperado, now the faithful servant and triumphant general of his king, wave the flag on all sides, crying in a loud voice: "Long live those high and mighty monarchs Ferdinand and Joanna of Castile, León and Aragón, in whose names and in favour of the royal Crown of Castile I take true, physical and lasting possession of all these seas and lands, coasts and harbours and islands, and I swear that should any prince or any other captain, Christian or heathen or of any other faith or rank whatsoever, lay claim to these lands and seas I will defend them in the name of the kings of Castile, whose property they are, now and for all time, as long as the world shall last and until the Day of Judgement."

All the Spaniards repeat this oath, and for a moment their words drown out the roaring of the waves. Each man moistens his lips with seawater, and once again the clerk Andrés de Valderrabáno takes note of this act of possession, closing his document with the words: "These twenty-two men, as well as the clerk Andrés de Valderrabáno, were the first Christians to set foot in the Mar del Sur, and they all tried the water with their hands, and moistened their mouths with it, to see whether it was salt water like the water of the other sea. And when they saw that it was so they gave thanks to God."

The great deed is done. Now they have yet to derive earthly benefit from their heroic undertaking. The Spanish plunder or barter a little gold with some of the natives. But a new surprise awaits them in the midst of their triumph, for the

Indios bring them whole handfuls of the precious pearls that are to be found on the neighbouring islands in rich profusion, including one, known as La Pellegrina, celebrated by Cervantes and Lope de Vega because, as one of the loveliest of all pearls, it adorned the royal crown of Spain and England. The Spaniards stuff all their pockets and sacks full of these precious things, which are not worth much more here than shells and sand, and when they greedily ask about what, to them, is the most important thing in the world—gold—one of the natives points south, to where the line of the mountains blurs softly into the horizon. There, he explains, lies a land of untold treasure, its rulers dine off golden vessels, and large four-legged animals—he means llamas—drag the most wonderful of loads into the king's treasury. And he tells them the name of the country that lies south in the sea and beyond the mountains. It is something like *Birù*, a strange and melodious sound.

Vasco Núñez de Balboa stares the way the man's hand is pointing, into the distance where the mountains disappear in the pallor of the sky. That soft and seductive word, *Birù*, has written itself at once on his soul. His heart thuds restlessly. For the second time in his life, he has found great, unhoped-for promise. The first message, Comagre's information about the nearby sea, has proved true. He has found the beach of pearls and the Mar del Sur. Perhaps the second message will be the same; perhaps he will succeed in discovering and conquering the Inca domain, the golden land of this earth.

THE GODS GRANT ONLY ONE IMMORTAL DEED

Núñez de Balboa is still staring into the distance with a longing gaze. The word *Birù*, "Peru", rings in his mind like a golden bell. But he knows—with painful resignation—that he cannot venture to find out more this time. You cannot conquer a kingdom with two or three dozen worn-out men. So first he must go back to Darién, and later, with all the forces he can gather, set out on the way he has now discovered to find the new Ophir. But the march back is as hard as the march out to find the ocean. Once again the Spaniards must fight their way through the jungle, once again they must repel attacks by the natives. And they are not a fighting unit now, but a small group of men sick with fever and staggering with the last of their strength—Balboa himself is near death, and has to be carried in a hammock by the Indios. After four months of terrible stress and strain, he gets back to Darién on 19th January 1514. But one of the great deeds of history has been done. Balboa has fulfilled his promise, all who ventured into the unknown with him are rich now; his soldiers have brought home from the coast of the southern sea treasures never known to Columbus and the other conquistadors, and all the other colonists get their share. One-fifth is put aside for the Crown, and no one begrudges the conqueror the fact that he treats his dog Leoncico like any other warrior as a reward for tearing the flesh from the bones of the unhappy natives, and presents him with 500 gold pesos. Not a man in the colony now quarrels with Balboa's authority as governor after such an achievement. The adventurer and rebel is honoured like a god, and he can prepare with pride to send Spain the news that he has performed the greatest deed for the Crown of Castile since Columbus. The sun of his good fortune, rising steeply, has broken through all the clouds that have loomed over his life until now. It is at its zenith.

But Balboa's happiness does not last long. On a radiant June day a few months later the astonished people of Darién flock down to the beach. A sail has been sighted on the horizon, and already it is like a miracle in this forsaken corner of the world. And look, a second sail appears beside it, a third, a fourth, a fifth; and soon there are ten, no, fifteen, no, twenty—a whole fleet making for the harbour. Soon everyone knows: all this is the work of Núñez de Balboa's letter, but not the letter with the news of his triumph—which has not yet reached Spain—but the earlier letter in which, for the first time, he described the native chief's account of the nearby southern sea and the land of gold, asking for an army of 1,000 men to conquer those lands. The Spanish Crown did not hesitate to equip such a mighty fleet for that expedition, but no one in Seville and Barcelona thought of entrusting so important a task to a rebellious adventurer with such a bad reputation as Vasco Núñez de Balboa. Their own choice of governor is sent. A rich, aristocratic and highly regarded man of sixty, Pedro Arias Dávila, usually called Pedrarias, comes with the fleet to act as the king's governor and restore order to the colony at last, do justice for all the crimes so far committed, find the southern sea and conquer the promised land of gold.

The situation is an awkward one for Pedrarias. On the one hand he has the mission of calling the rebel Núñez de

Balboa to account for his earlier hunting-down of the first governor, and if he is proved guilty putting him in chains or executing him; on the other, he has to discover the southern sea. However, as soon as his boat comes ashore he learns that this same Núñez de Balboa, whom he is to bring to justice, has done the great deed himself, that the rebel has already celebrated the triumph meant for him, and has done the Spanish Crown the greatest service since the discovery of America. Of course he cannot now put such a man's head on the block as if he were a common criminal; he must greet him courteously and offer honest congratulations. From this moment, however, Núñez de Balboa is lost. Pedrarias will never forgive his rival for having done the deed that he himself was to do, and that would have ensured his eternal fame through the ages. Of course, he must hide his hatred for their hero from the colonists for fear of embittering them too soon; the investigation is adjourned, and Pedrarias even makes a show of peace by betrothing his own daughter, whom he has left in Spain, to Núñez de Balboa. But his hatred and jealousy of Balboa are in no way mollified, only heightened when a decree arrives from Spain, where they have at last heard of Balboa's deed, bestowing a suitable title on the former rebel making him an Adelantado, and telling Pedrarias to consult him on every important matter. This country is too small for two governors; one will have to give way, one of the two must go under. Vasco Núñez de Balboa senses that the sword hangs over him, for military and legal power are in the hands of Pedrarias. So for a second time he tries flight, which served him so well the first time, flight into immortality. He asks

Pedrarias for permission to equip an expedition to explore the coast of the southern sea and conquer the land for a long way around. But the former rebel's secret intention is to make himself independent of any control on the other side of the sea, build his own fleet, be master of his own province and if possible also conquer the legendary Birù, that Ophir of the New World. Pedrarias cunningly agrees. If Balboa perishes in the attempt, all the better. If he succeeds, there will still be time to get rid of that over-ambitious man.

So Núñez de Balboa embarks upon his new flight into immortality, and the second is perhaps yet more magnificent than the first, even if the same fame has not been allotted to it in history, which honours only success. This time Balboa does not cross the isthmus only with his men. He has the wood, planks, sails, anchors and pulleys to build four brigantines dragged over the mountains by thousands of natives. Once he has a fleet over there, he can take possession of all the coasts, conquer the pearl islands and the legendary land of Peru. This time, however, fate is against the adventurer, and he keeps encountering new resistance. On his march through the moist jungle worms eat the wood, the planks rot and are useless. Not to be discouraged, Balboa has more trees cut down and fresh planks prepared on the Gulf of Panama. His energy performs true wonders—all seems to be going well, the brigantines are already built, the first in the Pacific Ocean. Then a sudden tornado floods the rivers where the ships lie ready. They are torn away and capsize in the sea. Balboa must begin again for the third time, and now at last he manages to complete two brigantines. Only two more, three more are needed now, and then he can set off and conquer the land of which he dreams day and night, ever since that native pointed south with his outstretched hand, and he heard, for the first time, the tempting name Birù. Recruit a few brave officers and good reinforcements for his crews, and he can found his realm! Only a few more months, only a little luck to go with his innate daring, and the name of the conqueror of the Incas would be known to world history not as Pizarro, the conqueror of Peru, but as Núñez de Balboa.

Even to its favourites, however, fate is not always generous. The gods seldom grant mortal man more than a single immortal deed.

DOWNFALL

With iron-hard energy, Núñez de Balboa has prepared his great enterprise. But the success of his audacity in itself puts him in danger, for the suspicious eyes of Pedrarias anxiously observe his subordinate's intentions. Perhaps news has reached him, through treachery, of Balboa's ambitions to rule his own province; perhaps it is just that he jealously fears a second success on the part of the former rebel. At all events, he suddenly sends Balboa a very friendly letter, asking him to come back to Acla, a town near Darién, for a discussion before he sets out on his voyage of conquest. Balboa, hoping to get more support from Pedrarias in the form of reinforcements, accepts the invitation and immediately turns back. Outside the gates of the town, a small troop of soldiers marches towards him, apparently to greet him; he joyfully goes to meet the men and to embrace their leader, his brother-in-arms of many years, his companion in the discovery of the southern sea, his great friend Francisco Pizarro.

But Pizarro lays a heavy hand on his shoulder and tells him he is under arrest. Pizarro too longs for immortality, he too longs to conquer the land of gold, and perhaps he is not sorry to know that so bold a predecessor will be out of the way. Pedrarias the governor opens the trial for alleged rebellion, and it goes ahead fast and in defiance of justice. A few days later Vasco Núñez de Balboa and the most loyal of his companions go to the block. The executioner's sword flashes, and in a second, as his head rolls, the first human eyes ever to see both the oceans that embrace our earth at the same time are extinguished for ever.

THE CONQUEST
OF BYZANTIUM

29 May 1453

THE DISCOVERY OF DANGER

On 5th February 1451, a secret messenger goes to Asia Minor to see the eldest son of Sultan Murad, the twenty-one-year-old Mahomet, bringing him the news that his father is dead. Without exchanging so much as a word with his ministers and advisers the prince, as wily as he is energetic, mounts the best of his horses and whips the magnificent pure-blooded animal the 120 miles to the Bosporus, crossing to the European bank immediately after passing Gallipoli. Only there does he disclose the news of his father's death to his most faithful followers. He swiftly gathers together a select troop of men, bent as he is from the first on putting an end to any other claim to the throne, and leads them to Adrianople, where he is indeed recognized without demur as the master of the Ottoman Empire. His very first action shows Mahomet's fierce determination as a ruler. As a precaution, he disposes of any rivals of his own blood in advance by having his young brother, still a minor, drowned in his bath, and immediately afterwards—once again giving evidence of his forethought and ruthlessness—sends the murderer whom he employed to do the deed to join the murdered boy in death.

In Byzantium, they are horrified to hear that this young and passionate prince Mahomet, who is avid for fame, has succeeded the more thoughtful Murad as Sultan of the Turks.

A hundred scouts have told them that the ambitious young man has sworn to get his hands on the former capital of the world, and that in spite of his youth he spends his days and nights in strategic consideration of this, his life's great plan. At the same time, all the reports unanimously agree on the extraordinary military and diplomatic abilities of the new Padishah. Mahomet is both devout and cruel, passionate and malicious, a scholar and a lover of art who reads his Caesar and the biographies of the ancient Romans in Latin, and at the same time a barbarian who sheds blood as freely as water. This man, with his fine, melancholy eyes and sharp nose like a parrot's beak, proves to be a tireless worker, a bold soldier and an unscrupulous diplomat all in one, and those dangerous powers all circle around the same idea: to outdo by far with his own deeds his grandfather Bajazet and his father Murad, who first showed Europe the military superiority of the new Turkish nation. But his initial bid for more power, it is generally known, is felt, will be to take Byzantium, the last remaining jewel in the imperial crown of Constantine and Justinian.

That jewel lies exposed to a fist determined to seize it, well within reach. Today you can easily walk through the Byzantine Empire, those imperial lands of Eastern Rome that once spanned the world, stretching from Persia to the Alps and on to the deserts of Asia, and it will take you only three days, whereas in the past it took many months to travel them; sad to say, nothing is now left of that empire but a head without a body—Constantinople, the city of Constantine, old Byzantium. Furthermore, only a part of that Byzantium still belongs to the emperor, the Basileus, and that is today's city of Istanbul, while Galata has already fallen to the Genoese and all the land beyond the city wall to the Turks. The realm of the last Roman emperor is only the size of a plate, merely a gigantic circular wall surrounding churches, the palace and a tangle of houses, all of them together known as Byzantium. Pitilessly plundered by the crusaders, depopulated by the plague, exhausted by constantly defending itself from nomadic people, torn by national and religious quarrels, the city cannot summon up men or courage to resist, of its own accord, an enemy that has been holding it clasped in its tentacles so long. The purple of the last emperor of Byzantium, Constantine Dragases, is a cloak made of wind, his crown a toy of fate. But for the very reason that it is already surrounded by the Turks, and is sacrosanct to all the lands of the western world because they have jointly shared its culture, to Europe Byzantium is a symbol of its honour. Only if united Christendom protects this last and already crumbling bulwark in the east can Hagia Sophia continue to be a basilica of the faith, the last and at the same time the loveliest cathedral of East Roman Christianity.

Constantine realizes the danger at once. Understandably afraid, for all Mahomet's talk of peace, he sends messenger after messenger to Italy: messengers to the Pope, messengers to Venice, to Genoa, asking for galleys and soldiers to come to his aid. But Rome hesitates, and so does Venice. The old theological rift still yawns between the faith of the east and the faith of the west. The Greek Church hates the Roman Church, and its Patriarch refuses to recognize the Pope as the greatest of God's shepherds. It is true that at two councils, held in Ferrara and Florence some time ago, it was decided that the two Churches should be reunified in view of the Turkish threat, and with that in mind Byzantium should be assured of help against the Turks. But once the danger was no longer so acute, the Greek synods refused to enforce the agreement, and only now that Mahomet has become Sultan does necessity triumph over the obstinacy of the Orthodox Church. At the same time as sending its plea for timely help, Byzantium tells Rome that it will agree to a unified Church. Now galleys are equipped with soldiers and ammunition, and the papal legate sails on one of the ships to conduct a solemn reconciliation between the two western Churches, letting the world know that whoever attacks Byzantium is challenging the united power of Christendom.

THE MASS OF RECONCILIATION

It is a fine spectacle on that December day: the magnificent basilica, whose former glory of marble, mosaic and other precious, shining materials we can hardly imagine in the mosque that it has now become, as it celebrates a great festival of reconciliation. Constantine the Basileus appears with his imperial crown and surrounded by the dignitaries of his realm, to act as the highest witness and guarantor of eternal harmony. The huge cathedral is overcrowded, lit by countless candles; Isidorus, the legate of the Pope in Rome, and the Orthodox patriarch Gregorius celebrate Mass before the altar in brotherly harmony, and for the first time the name of the

Pope is once again included in the prayers; for the first time devout song rises simultaneously in Latin and Greek to the vaulted roof of the everlasting cathedral, while the body of St Spiridon is carried in solemn procession by the clergy of the two Churches, now at peace with one another. East and west, the two faiths, seem to be bound for ever, and at last, after years and years of terrible hostility, the idea of Europe, the meaning behind the west, seems to be fulfilled.

But moments of reason and reconciliation are brief and transient in history. Even as voices mingle devoutly in common prayer in the church, outside it in a monastery cell the learned monk Genadios is already denouncing Latin scholars and the betrayal of the true faith; no sooner has reason woven the bond of peace than it is torn in two again by fanaticism, and as little as the Greek clergy think of true submission do Byzantium's friends at the other end of the Mediterranean remember the help they promised. A few galleys, a few hundred soldiers are indeed sent, but then the city is abandoned to its fate.

THE WAR BEGINS

Despots preparing for war speak at length of peace before they are fully armed. Mahomet himself, on ascending the throne, received the envoys of Emperor Constantine with the friendliest and most reassuring of words, swearing publicly and solemnly by God and his prophets, by the angels and the Koran, that he will most faithfully observe the treaties with the Basileus. At the same time, however, the wily Sultan is concluding an agreement of mutual neutrality with the Hungarians and the Serbs for a period of three years—within which time he intends to take possession of the city at his leisure. Only then, after Mahomet has promised peace and sworn to keep it for long enough, will he provoke a war by breaking the peace.

So far only the Asian bank of the Bosporus has belonged to the Turks, and ships have been able to pass unhindered from Byzantium through the strait to the Black Sea and the granaries that supply their grain. Now Mahomet cuts off that access (without so much as troubling to find any justification) by ordering a fortress to be built at Rumili Hisari, at the narrowest point of the strait, where the bold Xerxes crossed it in the days of the ancient Persians. Overnight thousands—no, tens of thousands—of labourers go over to the European bank, where fortifications are forbidden by treaty (but what do treaties matter to men of violence?), and to maintain themselves they not only plunder the nearby fields and tear down houses, they also demolish the famous old church of St Michael to get stone for their stronghold; the Sultan in person directs the building work, never resting by day or night, and Byzantium has to watch helplessly as its free access to the Black Sea is cut off, in defiance of law and the treaties. Already the first ships trying to pass the sea that has been free until now come under fire in the middle of peacetime, and after this first successful trial of strength any further pretence is superfluous. In August 1452 Mahomet calls together all his agas and pashas, and openly tells them of his intention to attack and take Byzantium. The announcement is soon followed by the deed itself; heralds are sent out through the whole Turkish Empire, men capable of bearing arms are summoned, and on 5th April 1453 a vast Ottoman army, like a storm tide suddenly rising, surges over the plain of Byzantium to just outside the city walls.

The Sultan, in magnificent robes, rides at the head of his troops to pitch his tent opposite the Lykas Gate. But before he can let the standard of his headquarters fly free in the wind, he orders a prayer mat to be unrolled on the ground. Barefoot, he steps on it, he bows three times, his face to Mecca, his forehead touching the ground, and behind him—a fine spectacle—the many thousands of his army bow in the same direction, offering the same prayer to Allah in the same rhythm, asking him to lend them strength and victory. Only then does the Sultan rise. He is no longer humble, he is challenging once more, the servant of God has become the commander and soldier, and his "tellals" or public criers hurry through the whole camp, announcing to the beating of drums and the blowing of trumpets that "The siege of the city has begun."

THE WALLS AND THE CANNON

Byzantium has only one strength left: its walls. Nothing is left of its once world-embracing past but this legacy of a greater and happier time. The triangle of the city is protected by a triple shield. Lower but still-mighty stone walls divide the two flanks of the city from the Sea of Marmara and the Golden Horn, but the defences known as the Theodosian walls and facing the open land are massive. Constantine, recognizing future danger, had already surrounded Byzantium with blocks of stone, and Justinian had further extended and fortified the walls. However, it was Theodosius who created the real bulwark with a wall seven kilometres long. Today the ivy-clad remains still bear witness to its stony force. Adorned with arrow slits and battlements, further protected by moats, guarded by mighty square towers, in double and triple parallel rows completed and renovated again and again by every emperor over 1,000 years, this majestic wall encircling the city is regarded as the emblem of impregnability of its time. Like the unbridled storm of the barbarian hordes in the past, and the warlike troops of the Turks now in the days of Mahomet, these blocks of dressed stone still mock all the engines of war so far invented; the impact of battering rams is powerless against them, and even shots from the new slings and mortars bounce off the upright wall. No city in Europe is better and more strongly defended than Constantinople by its Theodosian walls.

Mahomet knows those walls and their strength better than anyone. A single idea has occupied his mind for months and years, on night watches and in his dreams: how to take these impregnable defences, how to wreck structures that defy ruin. Drawings are piled high on his desk, showing plans of the enemy fortifications and their extent; he knows every rise in the ground inside and outside the walls, every hollow, every watercourse, and his engineers have thought out every detail with him. But he is disappointed: they all calculate that the Theodosian walls cannot be breached by any artillery yet in use.

Then stronger cannon must be made! Longer, with a greater range and more powerful shots than the art of war yet knows! And other projectiles of harder stone must be devised, heavier, more crushing, more destructive than the cannonballs of the present! A new artillery must be invented to batter those unapproachable walls, there is no other solution, and Mahomet declares himself determined to create this new means of attack at any price.

At any price... such an announcement already arouses, of itself, creative driving forces. And so, soon after the declaration of war, the man regarded as the most ingenious and experienced cannon-founder in the world comes to see the Sultan, Urbas or Orbas, a Hungarian. It is true that he is a Christian, and has already offered his services to Emperor Constantine; but, rightly expecting to get better payment for his art, and bolder opportunities to try it, he says he is ready, if unlimited means are put at his disposal, to cast a cannon for Mahomet larger than any yet seen on earth. The Sultan, to whom, as to anyone possessed by a single idea, no financial price is too high, immediately gives him as many labourers as he wants, and ore is brought to Adrianople in 1,000 carts; for three months the cannon-founder, with endless care, prepares and hardens a clay mould according to secret methods, before the exciting moment when the red-hot metal is poured in. The work succeeds. The huge tube, the greatest ever seen, is struck out of the mould and cooled, but before the first trial shot is fired Mahomet sends criers all over the city to warn pregnant women. When the muzzle, with a lightning flash, spews out the mighty stone ball to a sound like thunder and wrecks the wall that is its target with a single shot, Mahomet immediately orders an entire battery of such guns to be made to the same gigantic proportions.

The first great "stone-throwing engine", as the Greek scribes in alarm called this cannon, had now been successfully built. But there was an even greater problem: how to drag that monster of a metal dragon through the whole of Thrace to the walls of Byzantium? An odyssey unlike any other begins. A whole nation, an entire army, spends two months hauling this rigid, long-necked artefact along. Troops of horsemen in constant patrols thunder ahead of it to protect the precious thing from any accident; behind them, hundreds or maybe thousands of labourers work with carts to remove any unevenness in the path of the immensely heavy gun, which churns up the roads behind it and leaves them in a ruinous state for months. Fifty pairs of oxen are harnessed to the convoy of wagons, and the gigantic metal tube lies on their axles with its load evenly distributed, in the same way as the obelisk was brought from Egypt to Rome in the past. Two hundred men constantly support the gun on right and left as it sways with its own weight, while at the same time fifty carters and carpenters are kept at work without a break to change and oil the wooden rollers under it, to reinforce the supports and to build bridges. All involved understand that this huge caravan can make its way forward through the steppes and the mountains only gradually, step by step, as slowly as the oxen trot. The astonished peasants come out of their villages and cross themselves at the sight of the metal monster being brought, like a god of war escorted by its servants and priests, from one land to another. But soon its metal brothers, cast like the first in an original clay mould, are dragged along after it. Once again, human will-power has made the impossible possible. The round black muzzles of twenty or thirty such monsters are already pointing, gaping wide, at Byzantium; heavy artillery has made its first appearance into the history of war, and a duel begins between the 1,000-year-old walls of the emperors of eastern Rome and the new Sultan's new cannon.

THE ONLY HOPE

Slowly, laboriously, but irresistibly the mammoth cannon crush and grind the walls of Byzantium, their mouths flashing as they bite into it. At first each can fire only six or seven shots a day, but every day the Sultan brings up more of them, and with each hit another breach, accompanied by clouds of dust and rubble, is made in the stonework. It is true that by night the besieged citizens mend the gaps with increasingly makeshift wooden palisades and stop them up with bales of linen, but they are now not fighting behind the old impregnable walls, which had been hard as iron, and the 8,000 within those walls think with dread of the crucial hour when Mahomet's 150,000 men will mount their final attack on the already impaired fortifications. It is time, high time, for Europe and Christendom to remember their promise. Throngs of women with their children are on their knees all day in front of the shrines full of relics in the churches, soldiers are on the look-out from the watchtowers day and night to see whether the promised papal and Venetian reinforcement fleet will appear at last in the Sea of Marmara, swarming now with Turkish ships.

Finally, at three in the morning on 20th April, a signal flare goes up. Sails have been sighted in the distance—not the mighty Christian fleet that Byzantium had dreamt of, but all the same three large Genoese vessels are coming up slowly with the wind behind them. They are followed by a fourth, smaller, Byzantine grain ship that the three larger vessels have placed in their midst for protection. At once the whole of Constantinople gathers enthusiastically by the ramparts on the banks of the Bosporus to greet these reinforcements. But at the same time Mahomet flings himself on his horse and gallops as fast as he can from his crimson tent down to the harbour, where the Turkish fleet lies at anchor, and gives orders for the ships to be prevented at any cost from running into the Golden Horn, the harbour of Byzantium.

The Turkish fleet numbers 150 ships, although they are smaller vessels, and at once thousands of oars dip splashing into the sea. With grappling hooks, flamethrowers and slingstones those 150 caravels work their way towards the four galleons, but the four mighty ships, driven on fast by the wind, overtake and pass the Turkish boats spitting out missiles and shouting at the enemy. Majestically, with round sails swelling broadly and ignoring their attackers, the four steer towards the safe harbour of the Golden Horn, where the famous chain stretched across it from Stamboul to Galata is supposed to offer long-term protection against attack. The four galleons are very close to their destination now; the thousands on the walls can make out every individual face, men and women are already throwing themselves on their knees to thank God for this glorious deliverance, the chain in the harbour falls with a clatter to let the reinforcement ships in.

Then, all of a sudden, a terrible thing happens. The wind suddenly drops, and as if held by a magnet the four sailing ships are suddenly becalmed in the middle of the sea, only a stone's throw from the safety of the harbour. The entire fleet of enemy boats, their crews shouting jubilantly, fling themselves at the four crippled ships standing motionless in the water like four towers. The smaller vessels attach themselves with grappling hooks to the flanks of the large galleons, like hounds attacking a sixteen-tine deer, striking the wood of their hulls with axes to sink them, sending more and more men to climb the anchor chains, flinging torches and firebrands at the sails to set them alight. The captain of the Turkish armada drives his own flagship with determination against the transport ship of grain to ram it. Already the two ships are locked together. The Genoese sailors, higher up than the Turkish boats and protected by armoured foredecks, can fend off the climbing attackers at first, driving them away with axes and stones and Greek fire. But soon the fight must end; there are too many against too few. The Genoese ships are lost.

It is a dreadful spectacle for the thousands on the walls. As close as they are to the bloodthirsty fighting in the hippodrome, where they go for their own pleasure, they are now painfully close to a naval battle that they can watch with the naked eye and see the apparently inevitable downfall of their own ships. Two more hours at the most, and the four ships will be defeated by the enemy pack in the arena of the sea. Their helpers have come in vain, it was all for nothing! The despairing Greeks on the walls of Constantinople, only a stone's throw from their brothers, stand shouting, their fists clenched in helpless rage, unable to help their saviours. Many try to spur on their fighting friends with wild gestures. Others, hands raised to heaven, call on Christ and the Archangel Michael and all the saints of their churches and cloisters who have kept Byzantium safe for so many centuries, begging them to work a miracle. But the Turks on the opposite bank of Galata are themselves watching and shouting and praying just as fervently for their own people to be victorious: the sea has become a stage, the naval battle a gladiatorial contest. The Sultan himself has come up at the gallop. Surrounded by his pashas, he rides so far into the water that his coat is wet; and, shouting through his cupped hands as if to magnify his voice, he angrily orders his men to capture the Christian ships at all costs. Again and again, as a galley is driven back, he rages and threatens his admiral with his curved sword. "If you do not win this battle then don't come back alive."

The four Christian ships are still holding out. But the battle is approaching its end, the slingshots with which they are driving off the Turkish ships are running out, the sailors are tiring after hours of battle against an enemy who outnumbers them fifty times over. The day is nearly over, the sun is sinking to the horizon. Another hour, and the ships, even if the Turks have not captured them with grappling hooks by then, will be carried defenceless by the current to the bank beyond Galata, which is in Turkish hands. They are lost, lost, lost.

Then something happens that appears to the despairing, weeping, lamenting throng from Byzantium like a miracle. Suddenly a slight sound is heard, suddenly the wind is rising. And the slack sails of the four ships at once fill out, large and round. The wind that the Christians have longed and prayed for has reawakened. The bows of the galleons rise triumphantly, with a swelling thrust they overtake and outstrip their pursuers. They are free, they are safe. The first, then the second, the third, the fourth now run into the safety of the harbour to the roars of jubilation of thousands on the walls, the chain that has been lowered rises again, clinking, and behind them, scattered on the sea, the pack of smaller Turkish vessels is left powerless. Once again, the joy of hope hovers like a crimson cloud over the gloomy and desperate city.

THE FLEET CROSSES THE MOUNTAIN

The exuberant delight of the besieged citizens lasts for a night, and night always beguiles the senses with fantasy, confusing hope with the sweet poison of dreams. For the length of that night the besieged believe that they are secure and safe. For as those four ships have landed soldiers and provisions without mishap, more will come now, week after week, or so they dream. Europe has not forgotten them, and already, in their over-hasty expectations, they think of the siege as lifted, the enemy discouraged and conquered.

But Mahomet too is a dreamer, if a dreamer of that other and much rarer kind, one who knows how to transform dreams into reality. And even as the Genoese, in their delusions, think that they and their galleons are safe in the harbour of the Golden Horn, he is drafting a plan of such fantastic audacity that in all honesty it can be set beside the boldest deeds of Hannibal and Napoleon in the history of warfare. Byzantium lies before him like a golden fruit, but he cannot pluck it. The main reason is the Golden Horn, that inlet of the sea cutting deep into the land, a long bay that secures one flank of Constantinople. To penetrate that bay is in practice impossible, for the Genoese city of Galata, to which Mahomet has pledged neutrality, lies at the entrance, and from there the chain is stretched across to the enemy city. So his fleet cannot get into the bay by thrusting forward, and the Christian fleet could be attacked only from the inner basin, where Genoese territory ends. But how can he get a fleet into that inner bay? One could be built, but that would take months and months, and the Sultan is too impatient to wait so long.

It was then that Mahomet made the brilliant plan of transporting his fleet from the outer sea, where it is useless to him, across the tongue of land and into the inner harbour of the Golden Horn. The breathtakingly bold idea of crossing a mountainous strip of land with hundreds of ships looks at first sight so absurd and impracticable that the Byzantines and the Genoese of Galata take as little account of it in their strategic calculations as the Romans before them and the Austrians after them did of the swift crossing of the Alps by Hannibal and Napoleon. All worldly experience tells us that ships can travel only by water, and a fleet of them can never cross a mountain. But it is always the true sign of a daemonic will that it can turn the impossible into reality, and in warfare military genius scorns the rules of war, and at a given moment turns to creative improvisation rather than the old tried and trusted methods. A vast operation begins, one almost without an equal in the annals of history. In secrecy, Mahomet has countless wooden rollers brought and fixed to sleighs by carpenters. The ships are drawn up out of the sea and fixed to the sleighs as if on a movable dry dock. At the same time thousands of labourers are at work levelling out the narrow mule-track going up the hill of Pera and then down again, to make it as even as possible for traffic. To conceal from the enemy the sudden presence of so many workmen, the Sultan has a terrifying cannonade of mortars opened up over the neutral city of Galata every day and night; it is pointless in itself, and its only purpose is to distract attention and cover the movement of ships over the mountains and valleys from one body of water to another. While the enemy is occupied, suspecting no attack except from the land, the countless round wooden rollers, well treated with oil and grease, begin to move, and now ship after ship is hauled over the mountain on those rollers, drawn in its sleigh-like runners by countless pairs of oxen and with the help of the sailors pushing from behind. As soon as night hides the sight, this miraculous journey begins. Silent as all that is great, well thought out as all that is clever, the miracle of miracles is performed: an entire fleet crosses the mountain.

The crucial element in all great military operations is always the moment of surprise. And here Mahomet's particular genius proves its worth magnificently. No one has any idea what he plans—"if a hair in my beard knew my thoughts I would pluck it out," that brilliantly wily man once said of himself—and in perfect order, while the cannon ostentatiously thunder against the walls, his commands are carried out. Seventy ships are moved over mountain and valley, through vineyards and fields and woods, from one sea to another on that single night of 22nd April. Next morning the citizens of Byzantium think they are dreaming: an enemy fleet brought here as if by a ghostly hand, sailing with pennants hoisted and fully manned, in the heart of their supposedly unapproachable bay. They are still rubbing their eyes, at a loss to imagine how this miracle was worked, when fanfares and cymbals and drums are already playing jubilant music right under the wall of their flank, hitherto protected by the harbour. As a result of this brilliant coup, the whole Golden Horn except for the neutral space occupied by Galata, where the Christian fleet is boxed in, belongs to the Sultan and his army. Unobstructed, he can now lead his troops over a pontoon bridge against the weaker wall. The weaker flank of the city is thus under threat, and the ranks of the defenders, sparse enough anyway, have to stretch over yet more space. An iron fist has closed more and more tightly round the victim's throat.

EUROPE, HELP!

The besieged are no longer under any illusions. They know that if they are also attacked in the flank that has been torn open, they will not be able to put up resistance for long behind their battered walls, 8,000 of them against 150,000, unless help comes very quickly. But did not the Signoria of Venice solemnly agree to send ships? Can the Pope remain indifferent when Hagia Sophia, the most magnificent church in the west, is in danger of becoming a mosque of the unbelievers? Does Europe, caught in strife and divided a hundred times over by unworthy jealousy, still not understand the danger to western culture? Perhaps—so the besieged say, consoling themselves—the fleet coming to their aid has been ready for a long time, and hesitates to set sail only because it does not know their predicament, and it would be enough if someone made the Europeans aware of the monstrous responsibility of this fatal delay?

But how can information be sent to the Venetian fleet? Turkish ships are scattered all over the Sea of Marmara; to break out from Byzantium with the whole fleet would be to deliver it up to destruction, also weakening the defence of the city, where every single man counts, by withdrawing a few hundred soldiers. They decide to venture only a very small ship with a tiny crew. Twelve men in all—if there were any justice in history, their names would be as well known as those of the Argonauts for such an act of heroism, but not a single name has come down to us. An enemy flag is hoisted on the little brigantine. The twelve men clothe themselves in the Turkish fashion, with turbans or tarbooshes on their heads, so as not to arouse attention. On 3rd May the chain closing off the harbour is let down without a sound, and with a muted beat of oars the bold boat glides out under cover of darkness. Lo and behold, a miracle… unrecognized, the tiny vessel passes through the Dardanelles and into the Aegean Sea. It is the very extent of the crew's audacity that cripples the enemy. Mahomet has thought of everything but this unimaginable turn of events—that a single ship with twelve heroes aboard would dare such an Argo-like voyage through his own fleet.

But the disappointment is tragic: no Venetian sails appear on the Aegean. No fleet is ready to come to Byzantium. Venice and the Pope, everyone has forgotten the city; absorbed in parish-pump politics, they are all neglecting their honour and their oath. These tragic moments in history are repeated again and again: where the highest concentration of all united forces should be brought together to protect European culture, the princes and their states cannot abandon their petty rivalries even for a short span of time. To Genoa it is more important to outshine Venice, and Venice in turn feels the same about Genoa, rather than uniting against the common enemy for a few hours. The sea is empty. The brave crew desperately row their nutshell of a boat from island to island. But the harbours everywhere are occupied by enemies, and no friendly ship will venture into the war-torn area any more.

Now what is to be done? Several of the twelve, not surprisingly, have lost heart. Why take the dangerous route back to Constantinople? They cannot bring the city any hope. Perhaps it has already fallen; in any case, if they go back, either prison or death awaits them. However—and all credit to those heroes whose names go unknown!—the majority decide in favour of returning. They have been sent to deliver a message, and they must go home to report on the outcome, depressing as it is. So the little ship ventures on the way back through the Dardanelles alone, and then through the Sea of Marmara and the enemy fleet. On 23rd May, twenty days after setting out—by now in Constantinople all hope of seeing their ship again has been lost, and no one expects a message or their return—on 23rd May a few men on watch on the walls wave their banners, for a small ship, oars beating fast, is approaching the Golden Horn, and when the Turks, alerted by thunderous cries of joy from the besieged city, see in astonishment that this brigantine, boldly passing through their waters under a Turkish flag, is an enemy vessel they come up on all sides to intercept it just before it reaches the protection of the harbour. For a moment Byzantium, uttering cries of jubilation, still lives in the happy hope that Europe has remembered them, and this ship is sent ahead as a messenger. Only in the evening is the truth known: the news is bad. Christendom has forgotten Byzantium. The besieged citizens are alone, and if they cannot save themselves they are lost.

THE NIGHT OF THE STORM

After six weeks of almost daily fighting, the Sultan has grown impatient. His cannon have destroyed the walls in many places, but whenever he gives orders to storm the city the attackers have so far been repelled with much bloodshed. There are only two possibilities left for a military commander: either to raise the siege or, after countless attacks at single points, to order a full-scale operation to take the city by storm. Mahomet summons his pashas for a council of war, and his passionate will triumphs over all reservations. That great storm, which will finally decide matters, is to take place on 29th May. The Sultan prepares for it with his usual determination. A festival day is proclaimed; 150,000 men, from the first to the last, are to carry out all the festive customs prescribed by Islam, performing their ablutions seven times in the day, reciting the major prayers three times. All the powder and shot they have left is brought up for an intensified artillery attack to make the city ready to be stormed, and separate troops are given their positions. From morning to night, Mahomet does not allow himself an hour's rest. He rides all along the gigantic camp from the Golden Horn to the Sea of Marmara, going from tent to tent, encouraging all the leaders in person, inspiring the men. But as the good psychologist he is, he knows how to bring his 150,000 men to the highest pitch of their lust for battle, and he makes them a terrible promise, one that to his credit—or discredit—he will keep in every particular. His heralds proclaim that promise to the winds, with the sound of drums and fanfares: "Mahomet swears, by the name of Allah, by the name of Mohammed and the 4,000 prophets, he swears by the soul of his father Sultan Murad, by the heads of his children and by his sword, that after his troops have stormed the city they shall have the right to loot it as they like for three days. Everything to be found within its walls, household goods and possessions, ornaments and jewels, coins and treasure, the men, the women and the children shall belong to the victorious soldiers, and he himself will have no part in it except for the honour of having conquered this last bulwark of the eastern part of the Roman Empire."

The soldiers receive this dreadful proclamation with roars of jubilation. The loud noise of it swells like a storm, and the cry of *Allah il Allah* from thousands of voices reaches the frightened city. *Jagma, Jagma*—loot, loot! The word becomes a battle cry, with drums beating, cymbals and fanfares sounding, and by night the camp turns into a festive sea of light. Shuddering, the besieged see, from their walls, how myriads of lights and torches burn in the plain and on the hills as their enemies celebrate victory even before it is won with the sound of trumpets, pipes, drums and tambourines. It is like the cruelly loud ceremony of heathen priests before a sacrifice. But then, at midnight, all the lights are extinguished on orders from Mahomet, and the fervent roars from a thousand throats end abruptly. However, the sudden silence and the oppressive dark weigh down on the distraught listeners even more terribly than the frenetic jubilation of light and noise.

THE LAST MASS IN HAGIA SOPHIA

The besieged citizens do not need anyone to make an announcement, any defector from the enemy camp, to know what lies ahead. They know that orders have been given to storm Byzantium, and presentiments of the monstrous commitment of the Turks and their own monstrous danger loom over the entire city like a storm cloud. Although it is usually split into factions of religious strife, the population gathers together in these last hours—as always, only the utmost need creates such a spectacle of earthly unity. So that they will all be aware of what they have to defend—their faith, their great past history, their common culture—the Basileus gives orders for a moving ceremony. At his command, the people all assemble, Orthodox and Catholics, clergy and laymen, children and old men, forming a procession. No one is to stay at home, no one *can* stay at home, from the richest to the poorest they gather devoutly together in that procession to sing the *Kyrie eleison* as they pass through the inner city and then go along the outer walls. The sacred icons and relics are brought from the churches to be carried at the head of the procession, and one of those holy images is hung wherever a breach has been made in the walls, in the hope that it will repel the storming of the city better than earthly weapons. At the same time Emperor Constantine gathers all the senators, the noblemen and the commanders around him, to inspire them with courage in his last speech. He cannot, however, like Mahomet promise them unlimited plunder. But he describes the honour they can win for Christianity and the whole western world if they withstand this last decisive storm, and the danger if they are conquered by those who have come to burn and murder: Mahomet and Constantine both know that this day will determine the course of history for centuries.

Then the last scene begins, one of the most moving in Europe, an unforgettable ecstasy of downfall. Those doomed to death assemble in Hagia Sophia, still the most magnificent cathedral in the world at that time, a place abandoned by the faithful ever since that day of the fraternal alliance of the two Churches. The whole court gathers round the emperor, the nobles, the Greek and Catholic priests, the Genoese and Venetian soldiers and sailors, all in armour and carrying weapons, and behind them thousands and thousands of murmuring shadows kneel in silent awe—the people of the city with their backs bowed, in a turmoil of fear and anxiety—and the candles trying to rival the darkness of the vaulting overhead light up the crowd kneeling in prayer as if it were a single body. The soul of Byzantium is praying to God here. Now the Patriarch raises his voice strongly, urging them on, and the choirs answer him. Once more the holy and eternal voice of the west answers him in the music filling this place. Then one after another they go up to the altar, the emperor first of all, to receive the consolation of the faith, until the huge cathedral is filled to high in its vaulting by a constant surge of prayer. The last Mass, the funeral Mass of the eastern Roman Empire has begun, for the Christian faith has lived for the last time in Justinian's cathedral.

After this overwhelming ceremony, the emperor returns fleetingly to his palace once more to ask all his subjects and servants forgiveness for any wrong he has ever done them in life. Then he mounts his horse and rides—like Mahomet his great enemy at the same hour—from end to end of the walls, encouraging the soldiers. It is deep night now. Not a voice rises, not a weapon clinks. Moved to their very souls, the 1,000 wait inside those walls. They are waiting for the day and for death.

KERKOPORTA, THE FORGOTTEN DOOR

At one in the morning, the Sultan gives the signal to attack. The great standards are unfurled, and with a single cry of *Allah, Allah il Allah* 100,000 men fall on the city walls with weapons and ladders, ropes and grappling hooks, while all the drums are beaten at the same time, all the fanfares blare and the kettledrums are struck, cymbals and flutes mingle their high notes with human cries and the thunder of the cannon into a single sound like the roar of a hurricane. Pitilessly the irregular troops, the bashi-bazouks, are flung against the walls—their half-naked bodies serving the Sultan's plan of attack to some extent, but only as buffers intended to tire and weaken the enemy before the core troops are brought into action for the final storm. Whipped on, the bashi-bazouks charge the walls in the dark, climb the battlements, storm the fortifications again and again, for they have no way of escape behind them, they are worthless human material marked out only for sacrifice. The core troops are already standing ready, driving them on to almost certain death. The defenders still have the upper hand; their coats of mail withstand the countless arrows and stones that come their way. But their real danger—and here Mahomet's calculations were correct—is weariness. Constantly fighting against the light Turkish troops pressing forward, always moving from one point of attack to another, they exhaust a large part of their strength in the manner of defence forced upon them. And now—after two hours of skirmishing day is beginning to dawn—the second line of attack, the Anatolians, are storming forward, and the battle becomes more dangerous. For the Anatolians are disciplined warriors, well trained and also wearing coats of mail; moreover, they are present in superior numbers and are well rested, while the defenders have to protect first one and then another breach against the enemy's incursions. But still the attackers are being thrown back, and the Sultan must turn to his last reserves, the janissaries, a troop of picked men, the elite guard of the Ottoman army. He places himself at the head of 12,000 young and carefully chosen soldiers, the best in Europe at this time, and with a single battle cry they fling themselves on their exhausted adversaries. It is high time for all the bells in the city to be rung to summon to the walls the last men capable of fighting, for sailors to be brought from the ships now that the crucial battle is in progress. To the undoing of the defenders, a rockfall strikes the leader of the Genoese troop, the bold condottiere Giustiniani, who is taken to the ships severely injured, and his fall makes the energy of the defenders falter for a moment. But then the emperor himself comes up to prevent the Turks breaking in, and once again the storm ladders are fended off. Determination stands against ultimate determination, and for the span of a breath it seems that Byzantium is saved, the worst of its need has withstood the wildest attack. Then a tragic incident tips the balance, one of those mysterious moments that history sometimes brings forth in accordance with its unfathomable will, and at a stroke the fate of Byzantium is decided.

Something wholly improbable has happened. A few Turks have made their way through one of the many breaches in the outer walls, not far from the real point of attack. They do not venture to attack the inner wall, but as they wander aimlessly and full of curiosity between the first and second city walls they discover that one of the smaller gates in the inner-city wall, known as the Kerkoporta, has by some incomprehensible oversight been left open. In itself it is only a small postern gate, meant for pedestrians in times of peace while the larger gates are still closed. Simply because it has no military importance, its existence has obviously been forgotten in the general turmoil of the previous night. Now, to their astonishment, the janissaries find this door in the middle of the sturdy bulwark usefully open to them. At first they suspect some trick of war, for it is so absurd that—while otherwise thousands of bodies are piled outside every breach and gap, every gate in the fortifications, while boiling oil and spears rain down—the gate here, the Kerkoporta, stands open to the heart of the city as if on a peaceful Sunday. For safety's sake they call up reinforcements, and without any resistance at all a whole troop makes its way into the inner city, suddenly attacking the unsuspecting defenders of the outer wall from behind. A few fighting men become aware of the Turks behind their own ranks, and the fatal cry rises, more murderous than any cannon in every battle, the cry of a false rumour. "The city is taken!" The Turks pass it on, louder and louder. "The city is taken!" That cry breaks all resistance. The troops of mercenaries, thinking themselves betrayed, leave their posts to get down to the harbour and the safety of the ships in time. It is useless for Constantine to fling himself and a few loyal men against the intruders; he falls unnoticed in the midst of the turmoil, and not until next day will anyone know, from the sight of crimson shoes decked with a golden eagle in a pile of bodies, that the last emperor of the eastern Roman Empire has lost his life and his empire in the honourable Roman fashion. A mote of coincidence, the forgotten door of Kerkoporta, has decided the course of the world's history.

THE CROSS FALLS

Sometimes history plays with numbers. The looting of Byzantium begins exactly 1,000 years after Rome was so memorably looted by the Vandals. It is terrible to say that, true to the oath he swore, Mahomet the victor keeps his word. After the first massacre, he indiscriminately leaves houses and palaces, churches and cloisters, men, women and children to his men to be plundered, and like devils out of hell thousands of them race through the streets to get what they want ahead of someone else. The first to suffer are the churches where vessels of gold shine and jewels sparkle, and whenever the looters break into a dwelling house they hoist their banner over it, so that the next arrivals will know that the loot here has already been claimed. That loot consists not only of jewels, fabrics, money and portable goods; the women are goods for sale to seraglios, the men and children are bound for the slave market. The unfortunates who took refuge in churches are whipped out again, the old people are killed as useless mouths to feed and unsaleable ballast, the young ones, tied together like cattle, are dragged away, and along with robbery senseless destruction rages. What valuable relics and works of art the crusaders left, after indulging in what may have been an equally terrible episode of looting, are now wrecked by the victors, torn apart, valuable pictures are destroyed, wonderful statues smashed to pieces, books in which the wisdom of centuries, the immortal wealth of Greek philosophy and poetry were to be preserved for all eternity burnt or carelessly tossed aside. Mankind will never know the whole of the havoc that broke in through the open Kerkoporta in that fateful hour, or how much the intellectual world lost in the looting of Rome, Alexandria and Byzantium.

Only on the afternoon of the great victory, when the slaughtering was over, does Mahomet enter the conquered city. Proud and grave, he rides his magnificent steed past scenes of plundering without averting his gaze. He is true to his word and does not disturb the soldiers who won him this victory as they go about their dreadful business. But his way takes him first not to see what he has won, for that is everything; he rides proudly to the cathedral, the radiant head of Byzantium. For more than fifty days he has looked with longing up from his tents at the shining, unapproachable dome of Hagia Sophia; now, as the victor, he may walk through its bronze doorway. But Mahomet tames his impatience once more: first he wants to thank Allah before dedicating the church to him for all time. Humbly, the Sultan dismounts from his horse and bows his head down to the ground in prayer. Then he takes a handful of earth and scatters it on his head, to remind himself that he, too, is a mortal man who must not think too highly of his triumph. And only now, after showing his humility to God, does the Sultan rise, as the first servant of Allah to enter it, and walk into Justinian's cathedral, the church of holy wisdom, the church of Hagia Sophia.

Moved and curious, the Sultan looks at the wonderful building, the high, vaulted roof, shimmering with marble and mosaics, the delicate arches that rise from darkness into the light. This most sublime palace of prayer, he feels, belongs not to him but to his God. He immediately sends for an imam, who climbs into the pulpit and from there recites the Mohammedan confession of faith, while the Padishah, his face turned to Mecca, offers the first prayer to Allah, ruler of the worlds, heard in this Christian cathedral. Next day workmen are told to remove all signs of the earlier faith; altars are torn down, whitewash is painted over the mosaics showing sacred scenes, and the tall cross of Hagia Sophia that has spread its arms wide for 1,000 years to embrace all the sorrow in the world falls to the floor with a hollow thud.

The sound as it strikes the stone echoes through the church and far beyond, for the whole of the west shakes as it falls. The terrible news echoes on in Rome, in Genoa, in Venice; like menacing thunder it rolls to France, to Germany; and Europe, shuddering, recognizes that—thanks to its own unfeeling indifference—a fateful, destructive power has broken in through the fatal forgotten gate, the Kerkoporta, a power that will bind and cripple its own strength for centuries. But, in history as in human life, regret can never restore a lost moment, and 1,000 years will not buy back what was lost in a single hour.

THE RESURRECTION OF
GEORGE FRIDERIC HANDEL

21 August 1741

O N THE AFTERNOON of 13th April 1737 George Frideric Handel's manservant was sitting at the ground-floor window of the house in Brook Street, very strangely occupied. He had found, to his annoyance, that his supply of tobacco had run out, and in fact he had only to go a couple of streets away to buy more at his sweetheart Dolly's shop, but he dared not leave the house for fear of his lord and master, a hot-tempered man. George Frideric Handel had come home from rehearsal in a towering rage, his face bright red from the blood that had risen to it, the veins standing out like thick cords at his temples. He had slammed the front door of the house and now, as the servant could hear, he was marching up and down on the first floor so vigorously that the ceiling shook; it was unwise to be negligent in his service on days when he was in such a fury.

So the servant was seeking diversion from his boredom by puffing not elegant rings of blue smoke from his short clay pipe, but soap bubbles. He had mixed a little bowl of soapsuds and was amusing himself by blowing the brightly coloured bubbles out of the window and into the street. Passers-by stopped, bursting a bubble here and there with their canes in jest, they laughed and waved, but they showed no surprise. For anything might be expected of this house in Brook Street; the harpsichord might suddenly play loud music by night, you might hear prima donnas weeping and sobbing as the choleric German, falling into a berserk rage, uttered threats against them for singing an eighth of a tone too high or too low. The neighbours in Grosvenor Square had long considered Number 25 Brook Street a madhouse.

The servant blew his bright bubbles silently and persistently. After a while his skills visibly improved; the marbled bubbles grew ever larger and more thin-skinned, they rose higher and higher, floating more lightly through the air, and one even sailed over the low roof ridge of the house opposite. Then he suddenly gave a start of alarm, for a dull thud made the whole house shake. Glasses clinked, curtains swayed; something massive and heavy must have fallen on the floor above. The manservant jumped up and raced upstairs to the study.

The armchair in which his master sat to work was empty, the room itself was empty, and the servant was about to hurry into the bedroom when he saw Handel lying motionless on the floor, his eyes open and staring; and now, as the servant stood stock still in his initial panic, he heard heavy, stertorous breathing. The strong man was lying on his back groaning, or rather the groans were forcing their way out of him in short and increasingly weak grunts.

He's dying, thought the frightened servant, and he quickly knelt down to help the semi-conscious Handel. He tried to raise him and carry him to the sofa, but the huge man's body was too heavy, too great a burden. So he simply loosened the neckcloth constricting Handel's throat, and the stertorous breathing at once died away.

And now up from the floor below came Christof Schmidt, the master's secretary and assistant, who had just been copying out some arias. He too had been alarmed by the heavy fall. The two of them raised the weight of the man—his arms dangled limp, like the arms of a dead corpse—and laid him on the sofa with his head raised. "Undress him," Schmidt ordered the servant. "I'll run for the doctor. And splash water on him until he comes round."

Christof Schmidt ran out without his coat, wasting no time, and hurried down Brook Street towards Bond Street, waving to all the coaches that trotted sedately by and took no notice at all of the stout, panting man in his shirtsleeves. At last one of them stopped. Lord Chandos's coachman had recognized Schmidt, who flung open the carriage door, ignoring all the rules of etiquette. "Handel is dying!" he cried out to the duke, whom he knew to be a great lover of music and his beloved master's best patron. "I must find a doctor." The duke immediately told him to get into the coach, the horses were given a sharp taste of the whip, and they went to fetch Dr Jenkins from a room in Fleet Street where he was earnestly studying a urine sample. But he immediately drove with Schmidt to Brook Street in his light carriage. "It's all the trouble he's had that's to blame," lamented the secretary despondently as the carriage bowled along. "They've plagued him to death, those damned singers and castrati, the scribblers and the carping critics, the whole wretched crew. Four operas he's written this year to save the theatre, but his rivals hide behind the women and the court, and then they're all mad for that Italian, that accursed castrato, that affected howling monkey. Oh, what have they done to our poor Handel! He's put all his savings into the theatre, £10,000 it was, and now they come plaguing him with their notes of what he owes, hounding him to death. Never has any man done such wonderful work, never has any man given so much of himself, but this would break a giant's back. Oh, what a man! What a genius!" Dr Jenkins, detached and silent, listened.

Before they entered the house he drew on his pipe once more and knocked out the ashes. "How old is he?"

"Fifty-two," replied Schmidt.

"Not a good age. He's been working like an ox. But he's as strong as an ox too, so let's see what can be done."

The servant held the basin, Christof Schmidt lifted Handel's arm, and the doctor cut into the vein. A jet of blood spurted up, hot, bright-red blood, and next moment a sigh of relief issued from the grimly compressed lips. Handel took a deep breath and opened his eyes. They were still weary, faraway and unaware. The light in them was extinguished.

The doctor bound up his arm. There was not much more that he could do. He was about to stand up when he noticed that Handel's lips were moving. He came closer. Very quietly, it was little more than a breath, Handel croaked: "Over… all over with me… no strength… don't want to live without strength…" Dr Jenkins bent lower. He saw that one eye, the right eye, was staring while the other looked livelier. Experimentally, he raised Handel's right arm. It fell back as if dead. Then he raised the left arm. The left remained in its new position. Now Dr Jenkins knew enough.

When he had left the room Schmidt followed him to the stairs, anxious and distressed. "What is it?"

"Apoplexy. His right side is paralysed."

"And will—" Schmidt hesitated—"will he get better?"

Dr Jenkins ceremoniously took a pinch of snuff. He did not care for such questions.

"Perhaps. Anything is possible."

"But will he remain paralysed?"

"Probably, in default of a miracle."

But Schmidt, who was devoted to his master with every bone in his body, persisted.

"And will he—will he at least be able to work again? He can't live without composing."

Dr Jenkins was already on the stairs.

"No, he will never work again," he said very quietly. "We may be able to save the man, but we have lost the musician. The stroke has affected his brain."

Schmidt stared at him with such terrible despair in his eyes that the doctor himself felt stricken. "As I said," he repeated, "in default of a miracle. Not that I've ever seen one yet."

George Frideric Handel lived for four months, devoid of strength, and strength was life to him. The right half of his body remained dead. He could not walk, he could not write, he could not play a single note on the keyboard with his right hand. He could not speak; his lip hung crooked from the terrible stroke that had torn through his body, and the words that issued from his mouth were only a muted babble. When friends made music for him a little light came into his eyes, and then his heavy, unwieldy body moved like that of a sick man in a dream; he wanted to beat time to the rhythm, but his limbs were frozen in a dreadful rigidity, and his sinews and muscles no longer obeyed him. The once-gigantic man felt helpless, walled up in an invisible tomb. As soon as the music was over his eyelids fell heavily, and he lay there like a corpse once more. Finally the doctor, in despair—for the maestro was obviously incurable—advised sending the patient to the hot baths at Aachen, which might perhaps effect some slight improvement.

But under the frozen exterior, like those mysterious underground hot springs themselves, there lived an incalculable strength: Handel's will, the primeval force of his nature, which had not been touched by the destructive stroke and would not yet allow the immortal part of him to founder in the mortal body. The huge man had not given up, he still wanted to live, to work; and against the laws of nature his will worked a miracle. The doctors in Aachen warned him sternly not to stay in the hot baths for more than three hours at a time; his heart would not survive any longer period, they said, it could kill him. But his will defied death for the sake of life and his burning desire: to recover his health. To the horror of his doctors, Handel spent nine hours a day in the hot baths, and with his will his strength too grew. After a week he could drag himself around again, after a second week he could move his arm, and in a mighty victory of will-power and confidence he tore himself free from the paralysing toils of death to embrace life once again, more warmly, more ardently than ever before, and with that unutterable joy known only to the convalescent.

On the last day before he was to leave Aachen, fully in control of his body, Handel stopped outside the church. He had never been particularly devout, but now, as he climbed to the organ loft with the easy gait so mercifully restored to him, he felt moved by something ineffable. Experimentally, he touched the keys with his left hand. The notes sounded, rang clear and pure through the expectant room. Now he tentatively tried the right hand that had been closed and paralysed so long. And behold, the silver spring of sound leapt out beneath his right hand too. Slowly, he began to play, to improvise, and the great torrent of sound carried him away with it. The masonry of music towered miraculously up, building its way into invisible space, the airy structures of his genius climbed magnificently again, rising without a shadow, insubstantial brightness, resonant light. Down below, anonymous, the nuns and the worshippers listened. They had never heard a mortal man play like that before. And Handel, his head humbly bent, played on and on. He had recovered the language in which he spoke to God, to eternity, to mankind. He could make music, he could compose again. Only now did he feel truly cured.

"I have come back from Hades," said George Frideric Handel proudly, his broad chest swelling, his mighty arms outstretched, to the London doctor who could not but marvel at this medical miracle. And with all his strength, with his berserk appetite for work, the convalescent instantly and with redoubled avidity immersed himself in composition again. The battle-lust of old had returned to the fifty-three-year-old musician. We find him now writing an opera—his right hand, cured, obeys him wonderfully well—a second opera, a third, the great oratorios *Saul* and *Israel in Egypt*, he writes *L'Allegro, il Penseroso ed il Moderato*; his creative desires well inexhaustibly up as if from a long-dammed spring. But the times are against him. The queen's death halts theatrical performances, then the Spanish war begins, crowds assemble daily in the public squares, shouting and singing, but the theatre remains empty and debts mount up. Then comes the hard winter. Such cold falls over London that the Thames freezes over, and sleighs with bells jingling glide over the mirror surface of the ice; all the concert halls are closed at this sad time, for no angelic music dares defy such terrible frosts. Next the singers fall ill, performance after performance must be cancelled; Handel's financial difficulties grow worse and worse. His creditors are dunning him, the critics are scathing, the public remains silent and indifferent, and gradually the desperately struggling composer loses heart. A benefit performance has just saved him from imprisonment for debt, but what a disgrace, to buy back his life as a beggar! Handel becomes more and more reclusive, his mind grows darker and darker. Was it not better to have one side of his body paralysed than his whole soul? In the year 1740 Handel feels a beaten, defeated man once more. His former fame is dust and ashes. Laboriously, he puts together fragments of earlier works, now and then he composes some small, new piece, but the great river of music has dried up; and healthy though his body is again, its primeval force is gone. For the first time that giant of a man feels weary, for the first time the great warrior feels defeated, for the first time he senses the sacred stream of creativity failing and drying up in him, a stream that has flooded a world with music for thirty-five years. Once again he has reached the end, once again. And he knows, or thinks he knows in his despair, that this is the end for ever. Why, he sighs, did God let me rise from my sickbed if men are to bury me once more? It would have been better to die than wander through this empty world in the cold, a shadow of myself. And in his rage he sometimes murmurs the words of the one who hung on the Cross: "My God, my God, why hast thou forsaken me?"

A lost, a desperate man, weary of himself, doubting his power, perhaps doubting God too, Handel wanders London by night in these months. He does not venture out of the house until late, for during the day his creditors are waiting outside the door to catch him with their notes of his debts, and in the street the glances of scornful and indifferent mankind fill him with disgust. Sometimes he wonders whether to take flight, go to Ireland where they still believe in his fame—but alas, they have no idea how broken his strength is—or to Germany, to Italy; his inner chill might thaw again there, and, touched by the sweet south wind, melody might break from the ravaged rocky landscape of his soul once more. That is the one thing he cannot bear: the inability to create, to compose. He, George Frideric Handel, cannot bear to be defeated. Sometimes he stops outside a church, but he knows that words will not comfort him. Sometimes he sits in a tavern, but a man who has known the high intoxication, the pure and blissful delights of creation feels only repelled by crude distilled spirits. And sometimes he stares down from a bridge over the Thames at the silent river running black as night, and wonders whether it might not be better to cast off all his cares with one determined leap. If only he need no longer bear the burden of this void, the horror of loneliness, forsaken by God and man.

One night he had been wandering in this way again. It was the 21st of August 1741, and the day had been warm and sultry. The sky had weighed down on London as hazy and hot as molten metal, and only when night fell did Handel go for a little fresh air in Green Park. He had been sitting there wearily in the impenetrable shade of the trees, where no one could see him or plague him, for his weariness weighed him down like an illness; he was tired of speaking, writing, playing music, thinking, he was tired of feeling, he was tired of life. Why and for whom should he live? He had gone home, walking like a man drunk along Pall Mall and St James's, urged on by the one compelling idea of sleep: to sleep and know no more, to sleep his fill, for ever if he could. No one was still awake in the house in Brook Street. Slowly—oh, how tired he was, how weary they had made him in hounding him!—slowly he climbed the stairs, their wood creaking at every heavy step he took. At last he was in his study. He struck a spark and lit the candle on the desk; he did it without thinking, automatically, as he had done for years, preparing to set to work. For in the past—and a melancholy sigh involuntarily escaped his lips—he used to come home from every walk with a melody, a theme that he always hastily dashed down so as not to lose the idea in his sleep. But now the desk was empty. No music paper lay on it. The sacred mill-wheel stood still in the frozen mill-stream. There was nothing to begin, nothing to finish. The desk was bare.

Or no: not bare! Wasn't there something white and papery shining in the bright rectangle of light? Handel reached for it. It was a package, and he felt that it contained written papers.

He quickly broke the seal. A letter lay on top, a letter from the poet Jennens who had written the libretti for his *Saul* and *Israel in Egypt*. Jennens wrote to say that he was sending Handel a new poem, and he hoped the great genius of music, *phoenix musicae*, would look graciously on his poor words and carry them up on his wings through the ether of immortality.

Handel started as if something terrible had touched him. Did this Jennens too mean to mock him, a dead and crippled man? With a violent movement he tore the letter in two, threw the crumpled remains on the floor and stamped on them. "The blackguard! The scoundrel!" he bellowed; the uncouth fellow had probed his deepest, burning wound and pierced him to the quick, to the bitterest gall of his soul. Angrily he blew out the light, groped his way confusedly to his bedroom and flung himself on the bed; tears suddenly broke from his eyes, and his whole body trembled in the rage of his impotence. Woe to this world, where the robbed are mocked and the suffering tormented! Why appeal to him now that his heart was frozen and the strength had gone out of him, why demand another work from a man whose soul was numbed and whose mind was powerless? All he wanted now was to sleep, unfeeling as a beast, to be forgotten, to be no more! The disturbed, ruined man lay heavily on his bed.

But he could not sleep. There was a restlessness in him, whipped up by his anger like the sea by a storm, a malignant and mysterious restlessness. He tossed from left to right and then from right to left again, becoming ever more wakeful. Perhaps he should get up after all and look at the libretto? But no, what could words still do for him, a dead man? There was no comfort for a man whom God had allowed to fall into the abyss, removing him from the sacred stream of life! And yet a power was still throbbing in him, strangely curious, urging him on, and in his helplessness he could not resist it. Handel rose, went back into his study and once again lit the candle with trembling hands. Had not a miracle raised him once before from the paralysis of his body? Perhaps God knew of healing and comfort for the soul as well. Handel moved the light towards the written sheets of paper. *Messiah*, read the first page. Another oratorio! The latest had failed! But, restless as he was, he turned over the title leaf and began to read.

At the first words he started up. "Comfort ye," began the libretto. "Comfort ye!"—it was like magic, that phrase—no, not a phrase, it was an answer divinely given, the cry of an angel calling from the overcast skies to his despairing heart. "Comfort ye"—how the words resounded, how they shook his subdued soul, those creative, fertile words. Already, although he had hardly read it, hardly sensed it, Handel heard the phrase as music, as hovering, calling, rushing, singing notes. O joy, the gates were flung wide, he could feel and hear in music again.

His hands shook as he turned page after page. Yes, he had been called, summoned, every word entered into him with irresistible force. "Thus saith the Lord"—was that not spoken to him and him alone, was not the same hand that had struck him down now raising him from the earth in bliss? "And he shall purify"—yes, he was purified; all at once the darkness was swept from his heart, brightness had dawned, and the crystalline purity of resonant light. Who had lent such rousing verbal force to the pen of poor Jennens, the poetaster of Gopsall, if not he who alone knew the composer's need? "That they may offer unto the Lord"—aye, a flame of offering had been lit in the smouldering heart, a sacrificial fire leaping to the sky in answer, responding to that magnificent cry. It was spoken to him, to him alone: "Lift up thy voice with strength"—yes, lift it up with the power of the sounding trumpets, the surging chorus, the thunder of the organ, so that once again, as on the first day of creation, the Word, the sacred Logos, might wake mankind, all humanity, all those still despairing in the dark; for truly, "Behold, darkness shall cover the earth", and they know nothing yet of the bliss of redemption granted him in this hour. And no sooner had he read the cry of thanks than the music surged up in him, fully formed: "Wonderful, Counsellor, the Mighty God"—yes, praise him, the Wonderful, the Counsellor who acted to bring peace to the distraught heart! "And lo, the angel of the Lord came upon them"—aye, it had indeed come down into this room on silver pinions, had touched him and redeemed him. How could he not give thanks, rejoice and hail the Lord with a thousand voices in his own, his sole voice, how could he not sing and praise God, saying: "Glory to God in the highest!"

Handel's head was bent over the sheets of paper as if bowed by a stormy wind. All his weariness was gone. He had never before felt his powers so strongly, never before known the joy of creation streaming through him like this. And again and again the words poured over him like torrents of warm, redeeming light, each going straight to his heart, an invocation liberating him. "Rejoice greatly!"—as that magnificent chorus burst forth he involuntarily raised his head and his arms spread wide. "He is the righteous Saviour"—aye, and he, Handel, would bear witness to it as no mortal man ever did before, he would raise his testimony like a shining sign above the world. Only one who has suffered deeply knows joy, only one who has been through tribulations can guess at the ultimate mercy of forgiveness, and it is for him to bear witness to the resurrection before men, for his sake who died. When Handel read the words: "He was despised", sad memories returned to him, transformed into dark, oppressive sound. They had thought he was defeated, they had already buried him alive, hounding him with their mockery—"All they that see him, laugh him to scorn"—yes, they had laughed at the sight of him. "But there was no man, neither found he any to comfort him." No one had helped him, no one had offered comfort in his helplessness, but there came a wonderful power: "He trusted in God", and God had delivered him. "But thou didst not leave his soul in hell." No, God had not left his soul in the tomb of his despair, in the hell of his impotence, a man in bonds, cast out, no, God had called him once again to carry the message of joy to mankind. "Lift up your heads"—how that music broke forth from him now, a great command to proclaim the word of God! And suddenly he shivered, for there, in the hand of poor Jennens, he read: "The Lord gave the word."

He held his breath. Here was the truth, spoken by any chance-come human mouth: the Lord had given him the word; it had come down to him from on high. "The Lord gave the word"; yes, the word was his, the sound was his, the grace was his! And it must go back to God, be raised to him by the overflowing heart; it was every creative artist's duty and desire to sing his praise. Ah, to grasp and hold and raise and wield the word, to draw it out, extend it to the width of the world, embracing all the joy of being, as great as God who gave it—ah, to change the word, the mortal, transient word, back into a thing of eternity through beauty and endless ardour! And behold, there the word was written, there it rang out, a word that could be repeated and transformed for ever: "Hallelujah! Hallelujah! Hallelujah!" Ah, to bring all the voices of this earth together in that word, high and low, the firm voice of a man, the yielding voice of a woman, to make them abundant, enhance them and vary them, bind them and loose them in rhythmical chorus, send them up and down the Jacob's ladder of the scale, soothe them with the sweet sound of strings, rouse them with ringing fanfares, bring them to burst forth in the thunder of the organ: "Hallelujah! Hallelujah! Hallelujah!" Ah, to take that word and that thanksgiving, and make it into jubilation echoing back from this earth and rising to the Creator of the universe!

Tears blurred Handel's eyes, so mighty was the fervour in him. There were pages still to read, the third part of the oratorio. But after that "Hallelujah! Hallelujah!" he could read no more. The words of rejoicing filled his inner being, drew him out, expanding him, burned like liquid fire trying to flow, to stream out of him. And how that jubilation urged him and surged within him, for it wanted to break out, to rise and return to heaven. Hastily, Handel picked up his pen and began setting down notes, forming sign after sign with magical speed. He could not stop, it carried him away like a ship with all sail spread running before a stormy wind. The night around was silent, the humid darkness lay quiet over the great city. But the light poured out within him, and the room echoed, unheard, to the music of the universe.

When his manservant cautiously entered the room next morning, Handel was still sitting at his desk writing. He did not reply when his secretary Christof Schmidt timidly asked whether he could be any help in copying the music, just uttered a low and dangerous growl. No one ventured to approach him again, and he did not leave the study for three weeks. When they brought him food, he hastily broke off a few crumbs of bread with his left hand while the other went on writing. For he could not stop; it was as if some mighty inebriation had seized upon him. When he rose and walked up and down the room, singing aloud and beating time, there was a strange look in his eyes; when anyone spoke to him he started, and his answer was uncertain and confused. Meanwhile, his manservant was not having an easy time. Handel's creditors came demanding payment of his debts, the singers came asking for a festival cantata, messengers came inviting Handel to the royal palace; the servant had to turn them all away, for if he tried to exchange even a word with the composer, who was working so furiously, his incensed master's anger was vented on him like the rage of a lion. George Frideric Handel knew nothing of the time and the hour in those weeks, he made no distinction between day and night, he lived entirely in the sphere that measures time only by musical beat and rhythm, he moved only with the torrents that surged from him ever more wildly, ever more urgently as the work flowed closer to the sacred rapids of its conclusion. Absorbed in himself, he paced up and down the self-appointed dungeon of his study with pounding, rhythmical steps; he sang, he touched the harpsichord, then he sat down again and wrote and wrote until his fingers were sore; never in his life had he felt such surging creativity, never had he lived and suffered like this in music.

At last, after just three weeks—a space of time still incredible today and for all eternity!—at last, on 14th September, the work was finished. The word had become music; what was only dry, sere language before now blossomed and sang, never to fade. The miracle of the will had been worked by the inspired soul, just as the paralysed body had once worked the miracle of resurrection. It was all written down, formed and constructed, rising and unfolding in melody—just one word still remained, the last in the work: "Amen". And now Handel seized upon that "Amen", those two brief, quick syllables, to build them into a stairway of music reaching to the sky. He cast them from voice to voice in alternating chorus, he drew those two syllables out and wrenched them apart again and again, only to merge them anew into yet more ardent sound, and like the breath of God his fervour flowed into that concluding word of his great prayer, so that it was wide as the world and full of its abundance. That one, last word would not let go of him, nor would he let go of it either, building up the "Amen" in a magnificent fugue from the first vowel, the echoing A, the primeval first note, until it was a cathedral, full and resonant, with a spire reaching to the heavens, rising higher and higher, falling again and rising once more, and finally seized upon by the stormy organ, flung up over and over again by the power of the united voices, filling all the spheres, until it was as if the angels themselves joined in that paean of thanksgiving, and the rafters were splintered overhead by that eternal "Amen! Amen! Amen!"

Handel rose to his feet, with difficulty. The pen dropped from his hand. He did not know where he was. He saw nothing, he sensed nothing, all he felt was exhaustion, immense exhaustion. He was so dizzy that he had to lean on the walls. The strength had gone out of him, his body was tired to death, his mind confused. He groped his way along the wall as a blind man might. Then he fell on his bed and slept like the dead.

His manservant knocked softly at the door three times that morning. The maestro was still asleep; his closed face was motionless, as if carved from pale stone. At midday the servant tried to wake him for the fourth time. He cleared his throat noisily, he knocked loudly. But no sound could penetrate the immeasurable depths of that sleep, no word could fall into it. In the afternoon Christof Schmidt came to the servant's aid. Handel still lay motionless. Schmidt bent over the sleeping man, who lay there felled by weariness after his extraordinary feat, like a dead hero on the field of battle after gaining the victory. However, Christof Schmidt and the manservant knew nothing about the great deed and the victory; they felt nothing but alarm to see him lying there so long, so uncannily motionless; they were afraid he might have suffered another stroke. And when, for all their shaking, Handel still would not wake in the evening—he had been lying there sombre and still for seventeen hours—Christof Schmidt went for the doctor again. He did not find him immediately, for Dr Jenkins, making the most of the mild evening, had gone out to fish on the banks of the Thames, and when he was finally tracked down he grumbled about the unwelcome intrusion. Only when he heard that the patient was Handel did he pack up his rod and line, fetch his surgical instruments for the bloodletting that would probably be necessary—all this took a great deal of time—and at last the pony trotted off to Brook Street with the pair of them.

But there was the manservant, waving to them with both arms. "He got up!" he shouted to them across the street. "And now he's eating like six porters. He ate half a Yorkshire ham in no time at all, I've had to pour him four pints of beer, and still he asks for more."

Sure enough, there sat Handel like the Lord of Misrule before a groaning board; and just as he had made up for three weeks' worth of sleep in a night and a day, now he was eating and drinking with all the relish and might of his gigantic body, as if to restore all at once the strength he had put into his work during those three weeks. No sooner did he set eyes on the doctor than he began to laugh, and it gradually became a vast, an echoing, a booming, a hyperbolical laughter; Schmidt couldn't remember seeing a smile on Handel's lips in all those weeks, only strain and anger, but now all the primeval, dammed-up joyousness of his nature burst forth like waves crashing against the rocks, foaming and breaking in rolling sound—never in his life had Handel laughed in so elemental a way as now, when he saw the doctor arriving just as he felt better than ever before, and the lust for life poured roaring through him. He raised his tankard and waved it at the black-clad doctor in greeting. "Devil take me!" cried Dr

Jenkins in amazement. "What's come over you? What kind of elixir have you drunk? You're bursting with life! What happened to you?"

Handel looked at him with a smile, his eyes sparkling. Then he sobered down again. Slowly, he rose and went to the harpsichord. He sat down, and at first his hands passed over the keyboard without touching the notes. Then he turned, gave a strange smile, and softly, half speaking and half singing, began the melody of the recitative "Behold, I tell you a mystery"—the words from *Messiah*, and he began them in jest. But as soon as he brought his fingers down through the mild air the music carried him away. In playing, Handel forgot the others and himself as his own current of music swept him gloriously along. Suddenly he was back in the middle of the work, he sang, he played the last choruses which he had written as if in a dream, but now he heard them waking for the first time: "O death, where is thy sting?" He felt the music within him, he was full of the fire of life, and he raised his voice higher, he himself was the rejoicing, jubilant chorus, and on he played and on, singing, all the way to the final "Amen, Amen, Amen". The room was almost shattered by those notes, so forcefully and with such weight did he throw his strength into the music.

Dr Jenkins stood there as if benumbed. And when Handel finally rose the doctor remarked with awkward admiration, just for something to say: "Good heavens, I never heard anything like that before. You must have been possessed by the Devil!"

But at that Handel's face darkened. He too was astonished by the work itself and the grace that had come upon him as if in his sleep. He too felt humbled. He turned away and said so softly that the others could hardly hear it: "No, I think it was God who possessed me."

Several months later two well-dressed gentlemen knocked at the door of the house in Abbey Street, Dublin, at present rented by that distinguished visitor from London the great composer Handel. Respectfully, they put their request: during these last few months Handel had given the capital of Ireland the pleasure of hearing works more wonderful than had ever been performed in the country before. They had heard, they said, that he meant to stage the première of his new oratorio *Messiah* here too; it was no small honour that he did the city in planning to present his latest creation here, even before London heard it, and in view of the extraordinary nature of the concert large profits might be expected. They had come, they said, to ask whether the master, whose generosity was known to one and all, might not donate the takings of that première to the charitable institutions which they had the honour to represent.

Handel looked kindly at them. He loved this city because it had given him its own love, and his heart was open. He would be happy to agree, he said smiling, let them just tell him which institutions were to profit by the performance. "The Society for Relieving Prisoners," said his first visitor, a kindly, white-haired man. "And the sick in Mercer's Hospital," added the other. But of course, they said, this generous donation would be only the proceeds of the very first performance; profits from the others would still go to the master.

However, Handel dismissed this idea. "No," he said quietly, "no money for this work. I will never take money for it, never,

I am too much in the debt of another. It shall always go to the sick and the prisoners. For I was sick myself, and it cured me; I was a prisoner and it set me free."

The two men looked up in some surprise. They did not entirely understand. But then they thanked him profusely, bowed, and left to spread the good news in Dublin.

At last, on 7th April 1742, came the final rehearsal. The only audience present consisted of a few relations of the members of the chorus from both cathedrals, and to save money the auditorium of the Music Hall in Fishamble Street was only dimly lit. A couple here, a little group there sat dispersed in isolation around the hall on the empty benches, to hear the new work of the maestro from London; the large auditorium was befogged, dark, cold. But as soon as the choruses began to crash out like great cataracts of sound a strange thing happened. The separate groups involuntarily moved closer together on the benches, gradually forming a single dark block, listening spellbound, for everyone felt as if the unheard-of force of this new music was too much for individuals, as if it would carry them away on its tide. They moved closer and closer as if to listen with a single heart, hearing the confident Word like a single devout congregation, the Word that, spoken and shaped in so many different ways, rang out to them from the intertwining voices. They all felt faint before that primeval strength, yet they were blissfully caught up by it and carried away, and a tremor of delight passed through them all as if through a single body. When the "Hallelujah!" burst out for the first time it brought one man to his feet, and all the others rose too as if at a signal; they felt you could not remain earthbound in the grip of such power, and stood to bring their voices a little nearer to God, offering their veneration in his service. Then they went out to tell the news from door to door: a work of music had been written such as was never heard on earth before. And the whole city was agog with joyful excitement, eager to hear this masterpiece.

Six days later, on the evening of 13th April, a crowd gathered outside the doors of the hall. The ladies had come without hoops in their skirts, the gentlemen wore no swords, so that there would be room for more people; 700, an unprecedented number, crowded in, so fast had the fame of the work preceded it. But not a breath was to be heard when the music began, and the listeners fell very still. Then the choruses burst out with hurricane force, and hearts began to tremble. Handel stood by the organ. He had intended to direct and conduct his work, but it tore itself away from him, he lost himself in it, it became as strange to him as if he had never heard it before, had never made it and given it form, and once again he was carried away on his own torrent. And when the "Amen" was raised at the end his lips unconsciously opened and he sang with the choir, sang as he had never sung in his life before. But then, as soon as the acclamations of the others filled the hall with a roar of sound, he quietly went to one side to thank not the men and women who in turn wished to thank him, but the grace that had given him this work.

The floodgates were opened. The river of music flowed on in him again year after year. From now on nothing could bow Handel, nothing could force the resurrected man to his knees again. Once again the operatic society he had founded in London went bankrupt, once again his creditors came dunning him to pay his debts; but now he stood upright and survived all his trials; undeterred, the sixty-year-old strode on his way, passing the milestones of his compositions. Obstacles stood in his path, but he gloriously overcame them. Old age gradually undermined his strength, weakened his arms, gout afflicted his legs; but undaunted he wrote on and on. At last his eyesight failed; he went blind while he was writing *Jephtha*. But even with blind eyes, like Beethoven with deaf ears, he still wrote on, untiring, invincible, and ever humbler towards God the greater his earthly triumphs were.

Like all true and rigorous artists, he did not praise his own works. But there was one that he loved, *Messiah*, and he loved it out of gratitude because it had saved him from his own abyss, because in it he had redeemed himself. Year after year he performed the work in London, always donating the full proceeds, £500 each time, for the benefit of the Hospital: a man cured to those who were sick, a man set free to those still in bonds. And it was with the work that had brought him out of Hades that he wished to take his own leave. On 6th April 1759, severely ill and now seventy-four years old, he had himself led to the podium of Covent Garden again. There the blind man stood, a huge figure amidst his friends, among the musicians and the singers: with the light gone from his empty eyes he could not see them. But when the surging notes rolled like waves towards him with a great, rushing rhythm, when the rejoicing of certainty rang in his ears, a hurricane swelling from hundreds of voices, his weary face cleared and lit up. He swung his arms in time, he sang as gravely and devoutly with the choir as if he were standing, priest-like, at the head of his own coffin, praying with them for his salvation and the redemption of all. Only once, when the trumpets suddenly came in at the words "The trumpet shall sound", did he start, looking up with his blind eyes as if he were ready now for the Day of Judgement; he knew he had done his work well. He could come before God with his head held high.

Moved, his friends led the blind man home. They too felt it had been a farewell. On his bed, he was still quietly moving his lips. He would like to die on Good Friday, he murmured. The doctors were surprised and did not understand him, for they did not know that this Good Friday would be the 13th of April, the date when the heavy hand had struck him down, the date when his *Messiah* was first performed. On the day when all in him had died, he had risen again. Now he wanted to die on the day when he had risen again, in the certainty of another awakening to life eternal.

And sure enough, his unique will had power over death as well as life. On 13th April Handel's strength left him. He saw nothing now, he heard nothing, his massive body lay on the pillows motionless, a heavy, empty frame. But as the empty seashell echoes to the roaring of the sea, so inaudible music surged within him, stranger and more wonderful than any he had ever heard. Slowly, its urgent swell freed the soul from the weary body, carrying it up into the weightless empyrean, flowing in the flow, eternal music in the eternal sphere. And on the next day, before the Easter bells began to ring, all that had been mortal in George Frideric Handel died at last.

THE GENIUS
OF A NIGHT

THE MARSEILLAISE

---

25 April 1792

1792. For two months, then three months, the National Assembly of France has been in a state of indecision: should it back war against the coalition of emperors and kings, or should it argue for peace? King Louis XVI himself cannot make up his mind; he has a presentiment of the danger if victory goes to the revolutionaries, he also fears the danger if they are defeated. The various parties are also undecided. The Girondists want war in order to stay in power, Robespierre and the Jacobins champion the cause of peace in order to use the interim period to seize power for themselves. The situation becomes increasingly tense with every passing day, the newspapers wax eloquent, the clubs discuss it all at length, rumours are wilder and wilder, inciting public opinion to become more and more agitated. When a decision does come, therefore, it feels like a kind of liberation. On 20th April, the King of France finally declares war on the Emperor of Austria and the King of Prussia.

An electric, soul-destroying atmosphere has weighed down heavily over Paris during those days and weeks, but even more oppressive and threatening is the sultry mood of agitation seething all along the border. Troops have already assembled in every village, volunteers and members of the National Guard are being equipped in every town, every fortress is put into order, and in Alsace above all they know that, as usual in disputes between France and Germany, the first decision will be taken on Alsatian soil. On the banks of the Rhine the enemy, the adversary, is not such an indistinct emotional and rhetorical concept as in Paris, but part of the visible present perceived by the senses, for you can see the advancing Prussian regiments with your own eyes at the fortified bridgehead and from the cathedral tower. And by night you can hear the enemy's artillery carriages rumbling as they roll along, you can hear weapons clinking, and trumpet signals are blown across the river, which glitters in the moonlight as it flows indifferently on. Everyone knows that only a single word, a single decree is necessary to bring thunder and lightning spewing from the silent mouths of the Prussian cannon, showing that the thousand-year war between France and Germany has broken out again—this time in the name of a new kind of liberty on one side, and to shore up the old order on the other.

It is a unique day, then, that brings news of the declaration of war from Paris to Strasbourg on 25th April 1792. People immediately stream out of all the streets and houses into the open squares, the whole garrison marches off, regiment by regiment, for its final parade. In the main square Mayor Dietrich awaits them with a sash in the red, white and blue of the tricolour round his waist and the cockade on his hat, which he waves in a greeting to the soldiers. Trumpet fanfares and the beating of drums sound, calling for silence. Raising his voice, Dietrich reads the declaration of war out loud in both French and German, both here and in all the other city squares. After his last words die away, the regimental musicians strike up the first, provisional war song of the Revolution, the *Ça ira*, which is really a sparkling, high-spirited, mocking dance melody, but the thunderous sound of the regiments marching out with their weapons clinking lends it a martial air. Then the crowd disperses, taking the enthusiasm thus whipped up into all the alleyways and houses. Stirring speeches are made in the cafés and clubs, proclamations are made. *Aux armes, citoyens! L'étendard de la guerre est déployé! Le signal est donné!* They begin with these and similar cries, and everywhere, in all speeches and newspapers, on all posters, on all lips, rhythmical phrases are repeated—*Aux armes, citoyens! Qu'ils tremblent donc, les despotes couronnés! Marchons, enfants de la liberté!* Let the crowned despots tremble, such are their exhortations, take up arms, citizens, march on, children of liberty! And every time, the crowd repeats those fiery words with delight.

In the streets and squares, the huge throng is still rejoicing over the declaration of war, but at such moments of public jubilation other voices are also raised, quieter voices that do not entirely agree. Such a declaration also arouses fear and anxiety, but those voices whisper secretly indoors, or keep silent, pale-lipped. There are always mothers saying to themselves: won't the foreign soldiers murder my children? There are peasants in every country anxious for their possessions, their fields, their cottages, their cattle and the harvest. Won't the young seedlings be trampled down, won't their houses be plundered by the brutal hordes, won't blood be spilt in the fields that they cultivate? But the Mayor of Strasbourg, Friedrich Baron Dietrich, who is really an aristocrat, but like the best aristocracy of France at the time is devoted with all his heart to the cause of the new freedom, will let only the loud voices of confidence prevail. He deliberately turns the day of the declaration of war into a public festival. Sash across his chest, he hastens from one assembly to the next, spurring the people on. He has food and wine served to the soldiers as they march away, and that evening, in his spacious house on the Place de Broglie, he assembles the generals, the officers and the most important civil servants for a farewell party, making their enthusiasm seem like a triumphal celebration in advance. The generals, sure of victory as generals always are, preside over the evening, the young officers who see war as the purpose of their lives speak freely. Each encourages his comrades. They brandish their swords, they embrace and drink to one another, and over the good wine they make increasingly passionate speeches. "To arms, citizens! Let us march to save our native land! Those crowned despots will soon tremble! Now that the banner of victory is unfurled, the day has come to spread the tricolour all over the world! Now may every man do his best, for the king, for the flag, for freedom!" Their belief in victory and enthusiasm for the cause of liberty, they think at such moments, will weld the whole nation, the whole country, into a single sacred unit.

Suddenly, in the middle of all the talk and the drinking of toasts, Mayor Dietrich turns to a young captain from the corps garrisoning the fortress, Rouget by name, who is sitting beside him. He has remembered that this amiable officer—not exactly handsome, but likeable—wrote a very nice anthem six months before on the occasion of the proclamation of the constitution. The regimental director of music, Pleyel, set it to music at once. It was not a very demanding work, but had proved easy to sing; the military band had learnt it, it had been sung in choir in the open air of a square. Wouldn't the declaration of war and the march of the departing regiments be the right occasion for a similar celebration? So Mayor Dietrich casually asks, as you might ask a favour of a good friend, whether Captain Rouget (who without the slightest justification has ennobled himself, and is now Captain Rouget de Lisle) whether the captain wouldn't like to mark this patriotic moment by writing something for the troops as they march away, a war song for the army of the Rhine, which is to advance towards the enemy tomorrow?

Rouget, an unassuming, insignificant man who never thought much of himself—his poems have never been printed, his operas have been turned down—knows that occasional verse flows easily from his pen. He expresses himself ready to oblige this distinguished official, who is a good friend of his. Yes, he says, he will try. "Bravo, Rouget," says a general sitting opposite, raising his glass, and telling him to send the work straight after him to the battlefield—the army of the Rhine could do with a good, brisk marching song. Meanwhile another officer is launching into a speech. More toasts are proposed, there is more loud talk, more drinking. General enthusiasm washes like a strong wave over that minor chance exchange between Rouget and the mayor. The mood of the party is ever more ecstatic, louder, more frenetic, and it is some time after midnight when the mayor's guests leave his house.

The hour is late, after midnight. The 25th of April, so exciting a day for Strasbourg with the declaration of war, is over, and it is really the 26th of April now. Nocturnal darkness lies above the houses, but the darkness is illusory, for the city is still in a feverish state. In the barracks, the soldiers are getting ready to march, and behind closed shutters many cautious citizens may already be preparing for flight. A few platoons are marching down the roads, now and then you can hear clattering hooves as dispatch riders pass by, then a rumble again as a battery of heavy artillery comes up, and again and again you hear the monotonous call of the sentries communicating with each other. The enemy is too close, the mind of the city too unsure and agitated for anyone to sleep easily at such a crucial moment.

Rouget, who has now climbed the spiral staircase to his modest little room at 126 Grande Rue, is in a curious state of excitement himself. He has not forgotten his promise to try to write a marching song, a war song for the army of the Rhine, and do it as quickly as possible. He walks restlessly up and down in his small room. How to begin? All the stirring proclamations, the speeches, the toasts are still whirling chaotically around in his mind. "To arms, citizens!... March, children of liberty... we will crush all tyranny! The flag is now unfurled..." He also remembers other words heard in passing, the voices of women trembling for their sons, the peasants' concerns for the fields of France: will they be trampled, will blood be shed by foreign cohorts? Half unconsciously, he writes down the first two lines. They are only an echo, the repetition of the echo, and that cry:

> *Allons, enfants de la patrie,*
> *Le jour de gloire est arrivé!*

Arise, children of this land, the glorious day is here… then he stops and thinks. Yes, that will do. He has the beginning. Now to find the right rhythm, the melody to go with the words. He takes his fiddle out of the cupboard, he tries it. Wonderful: the rhythm fits the words perfectly in the very first bars. He hastily writes on, now carried away by the power that has entered into him. And suddenly it all comes together: all the feelings that are discharged in this hour, all the words that he heard in the street and at the mayor's banquet, hatred of tyrants, fear for his native land, love of liberty. Rouget does not have to compose poetry consciously; all he needs to do is put the words that went from mouth to mouth on this one day into rhyme, set them to the captivating rhythm of his melody, and then he has said and sung everything that the nation felt in its inmost heart. Nor does he have to compose the music deliberately, for the rhythm of the street and the hour comes in through the closed shutters, the rhythm of pride and the challenge in the marching steps of the soldiers, the sounding of the trumpets, the rumble of the cannon. Perhaps he does not hear it himself, not with his own ears, but the genius of the hour that, for this one night, has taken over his mortal frame has heard *him*. And the melody, ever more obediently, goes along with the joyful rhythm that is the heartbeat of a whole nation. As if he were taking dictation from a stranger, Rouget writes down the words and the notes more and more hastily—a storm has broken over him, such a storm as he never felt before in his limited bourgeois mind. It is an exaltation, an enthusiasm that is not his own; instead, a magical force concentrated into a single explosive second carries the poor dilettante 100,000 times beyond his own abilities, and flings him like a rocket up to the stars—a light and radiant flame burning for the space of a second. For one night, it was granted to Lieutenant-Commander Rouget de Lisle to be a brother of the immortals: out of the opening of the song, taken from the street and the newspapers, creative words form at his command and rise into a verse that, in its poetic expression, is as abiding as the melody is immortal.

> *Amour sacré de la patrie,*
> *Conduis, soutiens nos bras vengeurs!*
> *Liberté, liberté chérie,*
> *Combats avec tes défenseurs!*

Love of the fatherland, guide us, support our avenging arms… Then a sixth verse, the last, composed in emotion as a unified whole, combining the words perfectly with the melody, and the immortal song is finished before dawn. Rouget puts out his light and flings himself on the bed. Something, he does not know what, has raised him to a brilliance of the mind that he never felt before, and now something else flings him into dull exhaustion. He sleeps a sleep as deep as death. And the creative spirit, the poet, the genius in him has indeed died. But the completed work lies on the table, now released from the sleeping man, who was truly taken over by that miracle as if in a sacred frenzy. Hardly ever again in the history of all nations has a song so quickly and perfectly been made from words and music.

The same bells ring out from the cathedral to announce the new morning, as usual. Now and then the wind carries the sound of gunfire to the city from the River Rhine; the first skirmishing has begun. Rouget wakes up. With difficulty, he surfaces from a profound slumber. Something has happened, he vaguely feels, something has happened to him, although he has only a hazy memory of it. Only then does he notice the freshly written sheet of paper on the table. Verses? When did I write them? Musical notation in my own handwriting? When did I compose it? Oh yes—the song that my friend Dietrich asked for yesterday, the marching song for the army of the Rhine! Rouget reads his lines of verse, humming the melody that goes with them, but he feels, as the creator of a newly completed work always does, entirely unsure of himself. However, a military comrade is billeted next door to him; he shows his friend the song and sings it. His comrade seems to like it, merely suggesting a few small alterations. This first mark of approval gives Rouget a certain confidence. With all the impatience of an author, and proud to have kept his promise so quickly, he goes straight to the residence of Mayor Dietrich, who is taking a morning walk in his garden and mulling over a new speech. What, Rouget, you mean to say you've done it already? Well, let's have a rehearsal at once. The two of them leave the garden and go into the salon of the house. Dietrich sits down at the piano and plays the accompaniment, Rouget sings the words. Enticed by this unexpected music in the morning, the mayor's wife comes into the room and, trained musician that she is, immediately begins to work on setting the accompaniment so that it can be performed at a party for the friends of the family that evening, along with all kinds of other songs. Mayor Dietrich, proud of his pleasing tenor voice, says he will now study the song more thoroughly, and on the evening of 26th April, the day that saw the composition of its words and music in the early hours of the morning, it is performed for the first time in the salon of the mayor's house to an audience chosen at random.

They seem to have given it a friendly reception, and all kinds of civil compliments were probably paid to the author, who was in the audience himself. But of course the guests in the Hôtel de Broglie on the main square of Strasbourg have not the slightest idea that an eternal melody has descended, on invisible wings, into their earthly present. Contemporaries rarely grasp the true stature of a human being or a musical work on first acquaintance, and we can tell how little the mayoress was aware of that astonishing moment from a letter to her brother, in which she makes the miracle into a banal social event. "You know how many people we receive in this house, and we always have to think of some kind of new entertainment for them. So my husband had the idea of getting a song suitable for the occasion composed. The captain of the engineers' corps, Rouget de Lisle, a charming fellow who writes verse and composes music, swiftly provided the words and notation for a war song. My husband, who has a good tenor voice, sang the piece at once. It is very attractive, and shows certain unique qualities, having the good fortune to be livelier and more spirited than most such songs. For my own part, I turned my talent for orchestration to it, arranging the score for piano and other instruments, which gave me plenty to do. So the piece was played in our house, to the great satisfaction of the whole company."

"To the great satisfaction of the whole company"—that seems to us today surprisingly cool. But the merely friendly impression of mild approval is understandable, for at this first performance the *Marseillaise* cannot display its true force. The song is not a piece for a pleasing tenor voice, to be performed as a solo in a bourgeois salon as part of a programme of romances and Italian arias. It is a song that arouses listeners with the hammering, jaunty, demanding opening bars... *Aux armes, citoyens*... addressing a crowd, a great throng, and its true orchestration is for the clamour of weapons, fanfares blaring, regiments marching. And it is not for the audience at a polite recital, but for those involved, all fighting in the same struggle. It is not to be sung by a single soprano or tenor voice, it is for a crowd of 1,000, the very model of a marching song, a song of victory and death, a song of the singers' native land, the national anthem of an entire nation. The enthusiasm from which it was born will give Rouget's song the power that inspires it. It has not yet taken fire, the melody has not yet reached the nation's soul, the army does not yet know its marching song, its song of victory, the Revolution does not know its eternal paean.

Rouget de Lisle himself, the man who experienced that nocturnal miracle, has as little idea as the others of what he created in a single night, as if sleepwalking and led by a faithless genius. Of course that amiable dilettante is delighted to hear the invited guests applaud his work enthusiastically, to receive their civil compliments as its author. With the petty vanity of a petty mind he industriously tries to exploit this minor success in his small provincial circle. He sings the new tune to his comrades in the coffee houses, he has copies made and sends them to the generals of the Rhine army. Meanwhile, on orders from the mayor and at the recommendation of the military authorities, the regimental band stationed in Strasbourg has studied the *War Song of the Army of the Rhine*, and four days later, when the troops march away, the band of the Strasbourg National Guard plays the new march in the main square. The local Strasbourg publisher patriotically says that he is prepared to print the *Chant de guerre pour l'armée du Rhin*, which is dedicated respectfully to General Luckner by his military subordinates. But not one of the generals of the Rhine army thinks of having the new tune played or sung during the march itself, and so it seems, like all Rouget's efforts to date, that the salon success of *Allons, enfants de la patrie* is destined to remain a one day's wonder, a provincial matter, and as such to be forgotten.

But the innate power of a work cannot be hidden or fade away in the long run. Time can forget a work of art, can forbid it to be performed, leave it for dead and buried, but the elemental will always conquer the ephemeral. For a month, two months, nothing more is heard of the *War Song of the Army of the Rhine*. The printed and handwritten copies lie around or end up here and there, in hands indifferent to it. But if a work has truly aroused enthusiasm in a single human being, that is enough: genuine enthusiasm is creative in itself. At the other end of France, in Marseilles, the Club of Friends of the Constitution gives a banquet on 22nd June in honour of the volunteers marching away to war. Five hundred spirited young men sit at a long table in their new National Guard uniforms, and the atmosphere is as feverish as it was on 25th April in

Strasbourg, or indeed even more heated and passionate, thanks to the southern temperament of the people of Marseilles. And now they are not so vain and sure of victory as in that first hour after war was declared. For the war does not live up to the predictions of the generals, who had said that the revolutionary French troops had only to march straight over the Rhine to be welcomed everywhere with open arms. On the contrary, the enemy has made incursions far into French territory. The liberty of France is threatened, the cause of liberty itself in danger.

In the middle of the banquet one of the young men—his name is Mireur, and he is a medical student from Montpellier University—strikes his glass to call for quiet, and gets to his feet. They all fall silent and stare at him, expecting a speech, an address, but instead the young man raises his right arm in the air and strikes up a song, a new song unknown to them all, and no one knows how it came into his hands. *Allons, enfants de la patrie.* And this time the spark catches fire as if it had fallen into a keg of gunpowder. One man's emotion has touched another's; the eternal poles of feeling have come into contact. All these young men, who are setting out in the morning, prepared to fight for freedom and die for their native land, are aware that these words express their innermost will and their own true thoughts. The rhythm irresistibly carries them away into a unanimous ecstasy of enthusiasm. Verse after verse is hailed with jubilation, the whole song must be repeated once, then a second time, and now the melody is their own, they are singing, leaping to their feet in excitement, glasses raised, thundering out the refrain. *Aux armes, citoyens! Formez vos bataillons!* People come in from the street, their curiosity aroused, to hear the song that is being sung with such verve, and then they are singing it too. Next day the melody is on 1,000, 10,000 pairs of lips. A reprint spreads it further afield, and when the 500 volunteers march away on 2nd July the song goes with them. When they feel tired on the road, when their steps slow down, it takes only one man to strike up the anthem again and its irresistible rhythm gives them all new heart. When they march through a village and the peasants gather in amazement, when all the inhabitants assemble to see what is going on, they join in the chorus. It has become their song too. Without knowing that it was meant for the army of the Rhine, without any idea who composed it and when, the volunteers have adopted it as the hymn of their own battalion, bearing witness to their own life and death. It belongs to them, like their regimental banner, and, marching passionately ahead, they plan to carry it all over the world.

The *Marseillaise*—for that will soon be the name given to Rouget's song—wins its first victory in Paris. On 30th July the battalion marches through the suburbs, the banner and the song going ahead of it. Thousands, tens of thousands stand waiting in the streets to give them a festive welcome, and as the men of Marseilles advance, 500 of them singing in time with the song as if it rose from a single throat, singing it over and over again, the crowd listens. What kind of a wonderful, captivating song are the soldiers from Marseilles singing? What fanfare is it that goes to all hearts, accompanied by the beating of drums? *Aux armes, citoyens!* Two hours, three hours later, the refrain is being sung in all the streets of Paris.

The *Ça ira* is forgotten, so are the old marches, the worn-out couplets; the Revolution has recognized its own voice, the Revolution has found its song.

It moves on now like an avalanche in a victorious course that cannot be halted. The anthem is sung at banquets, in the theatres and clubs, then even in church after the *Te Deum*, and soon instead of the *Te Deum*. In a couple of months the *Marseillaise* has become the song of the French nation and the whole army. With his clever mind Servan, the first republican Minister of War, recognizes the tonic and exalting power of such a unique battle song. In short order, he gives orders for 100,000 copies to be distributed to all the detachments, and in two or three nights the song of an unknown composer has spread farther than all the works of Molière, Racine and Voltaire. Every party ends with the *Marseillaise*, every battle is preceded by the regimental musicians singing the song of liberty. At Jemappes and Neerwinden the regiments line up to the song for the final onslaught, and the enemy generals, who have no means of stimulating their troops but the old recipe of a double ration of brandy, see in alarm that they have nothing to set against the explosive power of this "terrible" hymn when it is sung by thousands upon thousands at the same time, storming like an echoing wave of sound against their own ranks. The *Marseillaise* now presides over all the battles of France, like Nike the winged goddess of victory, carrying away countless numbers into enthusiastic frenzy and to their deaths.

*

Meanwhile, an unknown captain of fortifications sits in the little garrison of Hüningen, busily designing ramparts and entrenchments. Perhaps he has already forgotten the *War Song of the Army of the Rhine*, the work he wrote long ago on the night of 26th April 1792, and does not dare to guess, when he reads what the gazettes have to say about that other anthem, the other war song that has taken Paris by storm, the victorious *Song of the Men of Marseilles*, that it is word for word and bar for bar the miraculous song that came to him and out of him on that night. For by a cruel irony of fate there is only one man who does not feel uplifted by its melody—roaring as it does to the skies, battering against the stars—and that is the man who wrote it. No one in all France troubles about Captain Rouget de Lisle, and the greatest fame that a song ever had is the song's alone; not a trace of it falls on its creator Rouget. His name is not printed on the text, and he himself would remain entirely unnoticed by the masters of the present hour if he had not irritated them by drawing attention to himself. For—a brilliant paradox of the kind that only history can produce—the creator of the revolutionary hymn is not a revolutionary himself; on the contrary, the man who did more than anyone else to promote the Revolution with his immortal song would like to dam it up again as firmly as possible. By the time the men of Marseilles and the Parisian rabble storm the Tuileries and depose the king, with his song on their lips, Rouget de Lisle has had enough of the Revolution. He refuses to take an oath on the Republic, and would rather leave the armed services than serve the Jacobins. The description of *liberté chérie*, beloved freedom, in his hymn is not an empty phrase; he hates the new tyrants and despots in the National Convention no less that he hated the crowned and anointed despots on the enemy side. He frankly vents his dislike of the Committee of Public Safety when his friend Mayor Dietrich, the godfather of the *Marseillaise*, with General Luckner, to whom it was dedicated, and all the officers and aristocrats who were present in the audience on the evening of its first performance, are dragged away to the guillotine. And soon a grotesque situation arises: the poet of the Revolution is imprisoned as a counter-revolutionary, he of all people is put on trial for betraying his native land. Only the 9th of Thermidor, opening the prisons on the fall of Robespierre, spared the French Revolution the shame of having handed over the author of its most immortal song to the "national razor".

However, it would have been a heroic death, and not such a pitiful twilight fate as lies in store for Rouget. For the unlucky man survives the one really creative day of his life by more than forty years, by thousands and thousands of days. He has been stripped of his uniform, his pension goes unpaid; the poems, operas and other texts that he writes are not printed or performed. Fate does not forgive the dilettante for forcing an entrance, unsummoned, into the ranks of the immortals. The little man lives out his little life by dint of working at petty and not always entirely honest businesses. Carnot and later on Bonaparte try in vain to help him. But something in the character of Rouget has been poisoned and distorted beyond redemption by the cruel chance that made him a god-like genius for three hours, and then scornfully cast him back into his own insignificance. He quarrels acrimoniously with all the authorities, he writes audacious and emotional letters to Bonaparte, who wanted to help him; he boasts openly of having voted against him in the constitutional referendum. His business involves him in dubious affairs, and he even becomes an inmate of the Sainte-Pélagie debtors' prison over the matter of an unpaid bill of exchange. Unpopular everywhere, hunted by his debtors, always in bad repute with the police, he finally hides somewhere in the provinces and, as if forgotten and departed in his grave, he listens there to the fate of his immortal song. He still remembers that the *Marseillaise* stormed all the countries of Europe with the victorious armies, that no sooner had Napoleon become emperor than he had it banned from all public musical programmes as being too revolutionary, and then the Bourbons had its performance entirely forbidden. Only with amazement does the embittered old man see how, after an age in human terms, the July revolution of 1830 resurrects his words and melody with their old force at the barricades of Paris, and the Citizen King, Louis-Philippe, grants him a small pension. It seems to the ruined and forgotten man like a dream that anyone still remembers him at all, but it is not much of a memory, and when he dies at last in 1836 in Choisy-le-Roi, when he is seventy-six, no one knows or can even give his name. Another human age must pass before the *Marseillaise*, by now well established as the national anthem, is sung again in the Great War at the French fronts in warlike conditions, and orders are given for the body of little Captain Rouget to be buried in the same place, the cathedral of Les Invalides, as the mortal remains of little Lieutenant Bonaparte. And so, at last, the creator of a famous song who was never famous himself lies in his native land's place of fame, resting after the disappointment of having been nothing but the poet of a single night.

LA MARSEILLAISE

Allons enfants de la patrie,
Le jour de gloire est arrivé!
Contre nous de la tyrannie,
L'étendard sanglant est levé, (bis)
Entendez-vous dans les campagnes
Mugir ces féroces soldats?
Ils viennent jusque dans vos bras
Égorger vos fils,
   vos compagnes!

Arise, children of the fatherland,
The day of glory has arrived!
Against us tyranny
Raises its bloody banner (repeat)
Do you hear, in the countryside,
The roar of those ferocious soldiers?
They're coming right into your arms
To cut the throats of your sons and
   women!

Aux armes, citoyens,
Formez vos bataillons,
Marchons, marchons!
Qu'un sang impur
Abreuve nos sillons!

To arms, citizens,
Form your battalions,
Let's march, let's march!
Let an impure blood
Water our furrows!

Que veut cette horde d'esclaves,
De traîtres, de rois conjurés?
Pour qui ces ignobles entraves,
Ces fers dès longtemps préparés? (bis)

What does this horde of slaves,
Of traitors and conjured kings want?
For whom are these vile chains,
These long-prepared irons? (repeat)

Français, pour nous, ah!
  quel outrage
Quels transports il doit exciter!
C'est nous qu'on ose méditer
De rendre à l'antique esclavage!

Aux armes, citoyens...

Quoi! des cohortes étrangères
Feraient la loi dans nos foyers!
Quoi! Ces phalanges mercenaires
Terrasseraient nos fiers
  guerriers! (bis)
Grand Dieu! Par des mains enchaînées
Nos fronts sous le joug se ploieraient
De vils despotes
  deviendraient
Les maîtres de nos destinées!

Aux armes, citoyens...

Tremblez, tyrans et vous perfides
L'opprobre de tous les partis,
Tremblez! vos projets parricides
Vont enfin recevoir leurs prix!
  (bis)
Tout est soldat pour vous combattre,
S'ils tombent, nos jeunes héros,

Frenchmen, for us, ah!
  What outrage
What fury it must arouse!
It is us they dare plan
To return to the old slavery!

To arms, citizens...

What! Foreign cohorts
Would make the law in our homes!
What! These mercenary phalanxes
Would strike down our proud
  warriors! (repeat)
Great God! By chained hands
Our brows would yield under the
  yoke
Vile despots would have themselves
The masters of our destinies!

To arms, citizens...

Tremble, tyrants and you traitors
The shame of all parties,
Tremble! Your parricidal schemes
Will finally receive their reward!
  (repeat)
Everyone is a soldier to combat you
If they fall, our young heroes,

La terre en produit de nouveaux,
Contre vous tout prêts à se battre!

Aux armes, citoyens...

Français, en guerriers magnanimes,
Portez ou retenez vos coups!
Épargnez ces tristes victimes,
À regret s'armant contre nous.
   (bis)
Mais ces despotes sanguinaires,
Mais ces complices de Bouillé,
Tous ces tigres qui, sans pitié,
Déchirent le sein de leur mère!

Aux armes, citoyens...

Amour sacré de la patrie,
Conduis, soutiens nos bras vengeurs!
Liberté, liberté chérie,
Combats avec tes défenseurs! (bis)
Sous nos drapeaux que la victoire
Accoure à tes mâles accents,
Que tes ennemis expirants
Voient ton triomphe et notre gloire!

Aux armes, citoyens...

The earth will produce new ones,
Ready to fight against you!

To arms, citizens...

Frenchmen, as magnanimous warriors,
You bear or hold back your blows!
You spare those sorry victims,
Who arm against us with regret.
   (repeat)
But not these bloodthirsty despots,
These accomplices of Bouillé,
All these tigers who, mercilessly,
Rip their mother's breast!

To arms, citizens...

Sacred love of the fatherland,
Lead, support our avenging arms!
Liberty, cherished liberty,
Fight with thy defenders! (repeat)
Under our flags, shall victory
Hurry to thy manly accents,
That thy expiring enemies,
See thy triumph and our glory!

To arms, citizens...

THE FIELD OF WATERLOO

NAPOLEON

---

18 June 1815

Destiny makes its urgent way to the mighty and those who do violent deeds. It will be subservient for years on end to a single man—Caesar, Alexander, Napoleon—for it loves those elemental characters that resemble destiny itself, an element that is so hard to comprehend.

Sometimes, however, very seldom at all times, and on a strange whim, it makes its way to some unimportant man. Sometimes—and these are the most astonishing moments in international history—for a split second the strings of fate are pulled by a man who is a complete nonentity. Such people are always more alarmed than gratified by the storm of responsibility that casts them into the heroic drama of the world. Only very rarely does such a man forcefully raise his opportunity aloft, and himself with it. For greatness gives itself to those of little importance only for a second, and if one of them misses his chance it is gone for ever.

GROUCHY

The news is hurled like a cannonball crashing into the dancing, love affairs, intrigues and arguments of the Congress of Vienna: Napoleon, the lion in chains, has broken out of his cage on Elba, and other couriers come galloping up with more news. He has taken Lyons, he has chased the king away, the troops are going over to him with fanatical banners, he is in Paris, in the Tuileries—Leipzig and twenty years of murderous warfare were all in vain. As if seized by a great claw, the ministers who only just now were still carping and quarrelling come together. British, Prussian, Austrian and Russian armies are raised in haste to defeat the usurper of power yet again, and this time finally. The legitimate Europe of emperors and kings was never more united than in this first hour of horror. Wellington moves towards France from the north, a Prussian army under Blücher is coming up beside him to render aid, Schwarzenberg is arming on the Rhine, and as a reserve the Russian regiments are marching slowly and heavily right through Germany.

Napoleon immediately assesses the deadly danger. He knows there is no time to wait for the pack to assemble. He must separate them and attack them separately, the Prussians, the British, the Austrians, before they become a European army and the downfall of his empire. He must hurry, because otherwise the malcontents in his own country will awaken, he must already be the victor before the republicans grow stronger and ally themselves with the royalists, before the double-tongued and incomprehensible Fouché, in league with Talleyrand, his opponent and mirror image, cuts his sinews from behind. He must march against his enemies with vigour, making use of the frenzied enthusiasm of the army. Every day that passes means loss, every hour means danger. In haste, then, he rattles the dice and casts them over Belgium, the bloodiest battlefield of Europe. On 15th June, at three in the morning, the leading troops of the great—and now the only—army of Napoleon cross the border. On the 16th they clash with the Prussian army at Ligny and throw it back. This is the first blow struck by the escaped lion, terrible but not mortal. Stricken, although not annihilated, the Prussian army withdraws towards Brussels.

Napoleon now prepares to strike a second blow, this time against Wellington. He cannot stop to get his breath back, cannot allow himself a breathing space, for every day brings reinforcements to the enemy, and the country behind him, with the restless people of France bled dry, must be roused to enthusiasm by a draught of spirits, the fiery spirits of a victory bulletin. As early as the 17th he is marching with his whole army to the heights of Quatre-Bras, where Wellington, a cold adversary with nerves of steel, has taken up his position. Napoleon's dispositions were never more cautious, his military orders were never clearer than on this day; he considers not only the attack but also his own danger if the stricken but not annihilated army of Blücher should be able to join Wellington's. In order to prevent that, he splits off a part of his own army so that it can chase the Prussian army before it, step by step, and keep it from joining the British.

He gives command of this pursuing army to Marshal Grouchy, an average military officer, brave, upright, decent, reliable, a cavalry commander who has often proved his worth, but only a cavalry commander, no more. Not a hot-headed berserker of a cavalryman like Murat, not a strategist like Saint-Cyr and Berthier, not a hero like Ney. No warlike cuirass adorns his breast, no myth surrounds his figure, no visible quality gives him fame and a position in the heroic world of the Napoleonic legend; he is famous only for his bad luck and misfortune. He has fought in all the battles of the past twenty years, from Spain to Russia, from the Netherlands to Italy, he has slowly risen to the rank of Marshal, which is not undeserved but has been earned for no outstanding deed. The bullets of the Austrians, the sun of Egypt, the daggers of the Arabs, the frost of Russia have cleared his predecessors out of his way—Desaix at Marengo, Kléber in Cairo, Lannes at Wagram—the way to the highest military rank. He has not taken it by storm; twenty years of war have left it open to him.

Napoleon probably knows that in Grouchy he has no hero or strategist, only a reliable, loyal, good and modest man. But half of his marshals are dead and buried, the others, morose, have stayed on their estates, tired of the constant bivouacking. So he is obliged to entrust a crucial mission to a man of moderate talent.

On 17th June, at eleven in the morning, a day after the victory at Ligny, a day before Waterloo, Napoleon gives Marshal Grouchy an independent command for the first time. For a moment, for a single day, the modest Grouchy steps out of the military hierarchy into world history. Only for a moment, but what a moment! Napoleon's orders are clear. While he himself challenges the British, Grouchy is to pursue the Prussians with a third of the army. It looks like a simple mission, straightforward and unmistakable, yet it is also pliable as a double-edged sword. For at the same time as he goes after the Prussians, Grouchy has orders to keep in touch with the main body of the army at all times.

The marshal takes over his command with some hesitation. He is not used to acting independently, his normal preference for circumspection rather than initiative makes him feel secure only when the emperor's brilliant eye tells him what to do. He is also aware of the discontent of the generals behind him, and perhaps he also senses the dark wings of destiny beating. Only the proximity of headquarters is reassuring, for no more than three hours of forced marching separate his army from the imperial troops.

Grouchy takes his leave in pouring rain. His men move slowly after the Prussians, or at least going the way that they think Blücher and his soldiers took, over the spongy, muddy ground.

THE NIGHT IN LE CAILLOU

The northern rain streams down incessantly. Napoleon's regiments trot along in the dark like a herd of wet livestock, every man with two pounds of mud on the soles of his boots; there is no shelter in sight, no house, not so much as a roof. The straw is too soggy for anyone to lie down on it, so groups of ten or twelve soldiers gather close together and sleep sitting upright, back to back, in the torrential rain. The emperor himself does not rest. His nervous febrility keeps him pacing up and down, for the men who go out to reconnoitre find the rain impenetrable, and reports brought back by scouts are at best confused. He still does not know whether Wellington will accept his challenge to give battle, and no news of the

Prussians has come from Grouchy yet. So at one in the morning, ignoring the cloudburst as the rain goes on, he is striding along the line of outposts to within firing range of the British bivouacs, which show a faint, smoky light in the mist now and then, and thinking about his plan of attack. Only as day begins to dawn does he return to the little hut in his shabby headquarters at Le Caillou, where he finds Grouchy's first dispatches: confused reports of the retreat of the Prussians, but at least there is the reassuring promise to keep following them. The rain gradually slackens. The emperor paces impatiently up and down his room and stares at the yellow horizon to see whether the terrain in the distance will be revealed at last—and with it his decision.

At five in the morning—the rain has stopped—his inner cloud, a cloud of indecision, also clears. The order is given: the whole army is to form up in rank and file, ready to attack, at nine in the morning. Orderlies gallop off in all directions. Soon drums are beating to summon the men. Only now does Napoleon throw himself on his camp bed to sleep for two hours.

THE MORNING OF WATERLOO

Nine in the morning, but the troops are not yet assembled in their full numbers. The ground underfoot, sodden after three days of rain, makes every movement difficult, and slows down the artillery as the guns come up. The sun appears only slowly, shining in a sharp wind, but it is not the sun of Austerlitz, radiant in a bright sky and promising good fortune; this northerly light is dull and sullen. But at last the troops are ready and now, before the battle begins, Napoleon rides his mare all along the front once more. The eagles on the banners bow down as if in a roaring gale, the cavalry shake their sabres in warlike manner, the infantry raise their bearskin caps on the tips of their bayonets in greeting. All the drums roll, the trumpets sound to greet their field marshal, but above all these sparkling notes, rolling thunderously above the regiments, rises the jubilant cry of *Vive l'empereur!* from the throats of 70,000 soldiers.

No parade in Napoleon's twenty-year reign was more spectacular and enthusiastic than this, the last of them. The cries of acclamation have hardly died away at eleven o'clock—two hours later than foreseen, two fateful hours later!—than the gunners are given the order to mow down the redcoats on the hill with case-shot. Then Ney, "the bravest of the brave", advances with the infantry, and Napoleon's deciding hour begins. The battle has been described a thousand times, but we never tire of reading the exciting accounts of its vicissitudes, whether in Sir Walter Scott's fine version or in Stendhal's episodic rendering. It is seen from both near and far, from the hill where the field marshals met or from the cuirassier's saddle, as a great incident, rich in diversity; it is a work of art with tension and drama brought to bear on its constant alternation of hope and fear, suddenly resolving into a moment of extreme catastrophe. And it is a model of a genuine tragedy, because the fate of Europe was determined in one man's destiny, and the fantastic firework of Napoleon's existence shoots up once more into the skies, before flickering as it falls and goes out.

From eleven to one o'clock, the French regiments storm the heights, take villages and military positions, are thrown back, storm into the attack once more. Ten thousand men already lie dead on the wet, muddy hills of the empty landscape, and nothing has been achieved but the exhaustion of the two adversaries. Both armies are tired to death, both commanders are uneasy. They both know that the victory will go to whichever of them gets reinforcements first, Wellington from Blücher, Napoleon from Grouchy. Napoleon keeps nervously raising his telescope, he keeps sending more orderlies out. If his marshal arrives in time, the sun of Austerlitz will shine over France again.

GROUCHY LOSES HIS WAY

Meanwhile Grouchy, unaware that he holds Napoleon's destiny in his hands, has set out according to his orders on the evening of 17th June, following the Prussians in the prescribed direction. The rain has stopped. The young companies who tasted gunpowder for the first time yesterday stroll along, as carefree as in peacetime; the enemy is still not in evidence, there is still no trace of the defeated Prussian army.

Then suddenly, just as the marshal is eating a quick breakfast in a farmhouse, the ground shakes slightly under their feet. They prick up their ears. The sound rolls over the country towards them with a muted tone that is already dying away:

they are hearing cannon, batteries of them, being fired far away, but not too far away. A march of three hours, at the most, will get them there. A few of the officers throw themselves down on the ground, in the style of American Indians, to get a clear idea of the direction the sound is coming from. That distant noise is constant and muted. It is the cannonade of Saint-Jean, the beginning of Waterloo. Grouchy holds a council of war. General Gérard, one of the commanders under him, a hot-headed and fiery soldier, wants them to make haste in the direction of the gunfire—"*il faut marcher aux canons*". A second officer agrees: they must get there as fast as they can. None of them is in any doubt that the emperor has attacked the British, and a fierce battle is in progress. Grouchy is not so sure. Used as he is to obeying, he sticks anxiously to his handwritten sheet of paper, the emperor's orders to him to pursue the retreating Prussians. Gérard becomes more insistent when he sees his superior officer's hesitation. "*Marchez aux canons!*" This time he makes it sound like a command, not a suggestion. That displeases Grouchy. He explains, more strongly and sternly, that he cannot deviate from his orders unless word comes from the emperor cancelling them. The officers are disappointed, and the cannon thunder on against the background of a hostile silence.

Gérard tries for the last time: he begs and pleads to be allowed at least to go to the battlefield with his division and some of the cavalry, pledging himself to be on the spot in good time. Grouchy thinks it over. He thinks it over for the length of a second.

THE HISTORY OF THE WORLD IN A MOMENT

Grouchy thinks it over for a second, and that single second shapes his own destiny, Napoleon's, and the destiny of the world. That second in a farmhouse in Walhain decides the course of the whole nineteenth century, and its immortality hangs on the lips of a very brave but very ordinary man, it lies flat and open in his hands as they nervously crumple the emperor's fateful order in his fingers. If Grouchy could pluck up his courage now, if he could be bold enough to disobey that order out of belief in himself and the visible signs he sees, France would be saved. But a natural subaltern will always obey the orders he was given, rather than the call of destiny.

And so Grouchy firmly declines to change their plan. It would be irresponsible, he says, to split up such a small corps even more. His orders are to pursue the Prussians, no more. He declines to act in defiance of the emperor's orders. The officers, in morose mood, say nothing. Silence falls round him. And in that silence the deciding second is gone, and cannot be recalled by words or deeds. Wellington has won. So they march on, Gérard and Vandamme with fists clenched in anger, Grouchy soon feeling ill at ease and less and less sure of himself with every hour that passes—for, strange to say, there is still no sign of the Prussians. They are obviously not on the route going straight to Brussels, and messengers soon report suspicious signs that their retreat has turned into a flanking march to the battlefield. There would still be time to put on a last quick spurt and come to the emperor's aid, and Grouchy waits with increasing impatience for the message bringing an order to go back. But no news comes. Only the muted sound of the cannon thunders over the shaking ground, but from farther and farther away: the guns are casting the iron dice of Waterloo.

THE AFTERNOON OF WATERLOO

By now it is one o'clock. It is true that four attacks have been repulsed, but they have done considerable damage to the emperor's centre; Napoleon is already preparing for the crucial storm. He has the batteries in front of La Belle-Alliance reinforced, and before the cannonade lowers its cloudy curtain between the hills, Napoleon casts one last glance over the battlefield.

Looking to the north-east, he sees a dark shadow moving forward as if it were flowing out of the woods: more troops! At once he turns his telescope that way; is it Grouchy who has boldly exceeded his orders and now, miraculously, is arriving at just the right moment? No, says a prisoner who has been brought in, it is the advance guard of General von Blücher's army. Prussian troops are on their way. For the first time, the emperor realizes that the defeated Prussians must have eluded pursuit to join the British early, while a third of his own troops are manoeuvring uselessly in open country. He immediately writes Grouchy a letter telling him at all costs to keep in contact with the Prussians and prevent them from joining the battle.

At the same time Marshal Ney receives the order to attack. Wellington must be repelled before the Prussians arrive. No risk seems too great to take now that the chances are so suddenly reduced. All afternoon ferocious attacks on the plateau go on, and the infantry are always thrown back again. Again they storm the ruined villages, again and again they are smashed to the ground, again and again the wave of infantrymen rises, banners fluttering, to advance on the squares of their adversaries. Wellington still stands firm, and still there is no news of Grouchy. "Where is Grouchy? Where can he be?" murmurs the emperor nervously as he sees the Prussian advance guard gradually gaining ground. The commanding officers under him are also feeling impatient. And, determined to bring the battle to a violent end, Marshal Ney—as recklessly bold as Grouchy is over-thoughtful (three horses have already been shot under him)—stakes everything on throwing the entire French cavalry into action in a single attack. Ten thousand cuirassiers and dragoons attempt that terrible ride of death, smashing through the squares, cutting down the gunners, scattering the rows of men in front. They in turn are repelled again, true, but the force of the British army is failing, the fist holding those hills tightly in its grasp is beginning to slacken. And now, as the decimated French cavalry gives ground, Napoleon's last reserve troops, the Old Guard, move forward heavily, slow of step, to storm the hill whose possession will guarantee the fate of Europe.

THE MOMENT OF DECISION

Four hundred cannon have been thundering without a break since morning on both sides. At the front, the cavalcades of horsemen clash with the firing squares, drumsticks come down hard on the drumheads, the whole plain is shaking with the noise. But above the battle, on the two hills, the field marshals are listening to a softer sound above the human storm.

Above the stormy crowds, two watches are ticking quietly like birds' hearts in their hands. Both Napoleon and Wellington keep reaching for their chronometers and counting the hours and minutes that must bring those last, crucial reinforcements to their aid. Wellington knows that Blücher is near, Napoleon is hoping for Grouchy. Neither of them has any other reserves, and whoever brings his troops first has decided the course of the battle. Both commanders are looking through telescopes at the outskirts of the woods, where the Prussian vanguard begins to appear in the form of a light cloud. But are those only a few men skirmishing, or the army itself in flight from Grouchy? The British are putting up their final resistance, but the French troops too are weary. Gasping like two wrestlers, the troops face each other with arms already tired, getting their breath back before they attack one another for the last time. The irrevocable moment of decision has come.

Now, at last, the thunder of cannon is heard on the Prussian flank, with skirmishing and rifle fire from the fusiliers. "*Enfin Grouchy!*" Grouchy at last! Napoleon breathes a sigh of relief. Trusting that his flank is now secure, Napoleon gathers together the last of his men and throws them once more against Wellington's centre, to break the defensive wall outside Brussels and blow open the gateway to Europe.

But the gunfire was only part of a mistaken skirmishing that the approaching Prussians, confused by the uniform of the men they take for enemies, have begun against the Hanoverians. Realizing their mistake, they soon stop firing, and now the massed crowd of them—broad, powerful, unimpeded—pours out of the wood. It is not Grouchy advancing with his troops, but Blücher, and with him Napoleon's undoing. The news spreads fast among the imperial troops, who begin to fall back, still in reasonably good order. Wellington, however, seizes this critical moment. Riding to the edge of the victoriously defended hill, he raises his hat and waves it above his head at the retreating enemy. His own men immediately understand the triumphant gesture. All at once what are left of his troops rise and fling themselves on the enemy, now in disarray. At the same time the Prussian cavalry charge the exhausted and shattered French army. The mortal cry goes up, "*Sauve qui peut!*" Within a few minutes the Grande Armée is nothing but a torrential stream of terrified men in flight, carrying everything along with it, even Napoleon himself. The cavalry, spurring their horses on, make their way into this swiftly retreating stream, easily fishing Napoleon's carriage, the army treasury and all the artillery pieces out of that screaming foam of fear and horror, and only nightfall saves the emperor's life and liberty. But the man who, at midnight, soiled and numb, drops into a chair in a low-built village inn is no emperor now. His empire, his dynasty, his destiny are all over: a small and insignificant man's lack of courage has destroyed what the boldest and most far-sighted of adventurers built up in twenty heroic years.

RETURN TO DAILY LIFE

As soon as the British attack has struck Napoleon down, a man then almost unknown is speeding in a fast barouche along the road to Brussels and from Brussels to the sea, where a ship is waiting. He sails to London, arriving there before the government's couriers; and, thanks to the news that has not yet broken, he manages to make a fortune on the Stock Exchange. His name is Rothschild, and with this stroke of genius he founds another empire, a family dynasty. Next day England knows about the victory, and in Paris Fouché, always the traitor, knows about the defeat. The bells of victory are pealing in Brussels and Germany.

Next morning only one man still knows nothing about Waterloo, although he was only four hours' march away from that fateful battlefield: the unfortunate Grouchy. Persistently and according to his orders, he has been following the Prussians—but, strange to say, has found them nowhere, which makes him feel uncertain. Meanwhile the cannon sound louder and louder, as if crying out for help. They feel the ground shake, they feel every shot in their hearts. Everyone knows now that this is not skirmishing, that a gigantic battle is in progress, the deciding battle.

Grouchy rides nervously between his officers. They avoid discussing the situation with him; he rejected their advice.

So it is a blessed release when they reach Wavre and finally come upon a single Prussian corps, part of Blücher's rearguard. Grouchy's men storm the Prussians barring their way. Gérard is ahead of them, as if he were searching for death, driven on by dark forebodings. A bullet cuts him down, and the loudest of those who admonished Grouchy is silent now. At nightfall they storm the village, but they sense that this small victory over the rearguard means nothing now, for suddenly all is silent from over on the battlefield. Alarmingly silent, dreadfully peaceful, a dead and ghastly quiet. And they all feel that the gunfire was better than this nerve-racking uncertainty. The battle must be over, the battle of Waterloo from where Grouchy—too late!—has received Napoleon's note urging him to come to the emperor's aid. It must be over, but who has won? They wait all night, in vain. No message comes from the battlefield. It is as if the Grande Armée had forgotten them and they were empty, pointless figures in impenetrable space. In the morning they strike camp and begin marching again, tired to death and long ago aware that all their marching and manoeuvring has been for nothing.

Then at last, at ten in the morning, an officer from the General Staff comes thundering towards them. They help him down from his horse and fire questions at him. But the officer, his face ravaged by horror, his hair wet at the temples, and trembling with the superhuman effort he has made, only stammers incomprehensible words—words that they do not, cannot, will not understand. They think he must be drunk or deranged when he says there is no emperor any more, no imperial army, France is lost. Gradually, however, they get the whole truth out of him, the devastating account that paralyses them with mortal fear. Grouchy stands there, pale and trembling as he leans on his sword. He knows that his martyrdom is beginning, but he firmly takes all the blame on himself, a thankless task. The hesitant subordinate officer who failed to make that invisible decision at the fateful moment now, face to face with nearby danger, becomes a man again and almost a hero. He immediately assembles all the officers and—with tears of anger and grief in his eyes—makes a short speech in which he both justifies and bewails his hesitation. The officers who still bore him resentment yesterday hear him in silence. Any of them could blame him and boast of having held a better opinion. But none of them dares or wants to do so. They say nothing for a long time, their depth of mourning silences them all.

And it is in that hour, after missing the vital second of decision, that Grouchy shows—but too late now—all his military strength. All his great virtues, circumspection, efficiency, caution and conscientiousness, are obvious now that he trusts himself again and not a written order. Surrounded by superior strength five times greater than his own, he leads his troops back again right through the middle of the enemy—a masterly tactical achievement—without losing a single cannon or a single man, and saves its last army for France and the empire. But when he comes home there is no emperor to thank him, and no enemy against whom he can lead the troops. He has come too late, for ever too late, and even if outwardly his life takes an upward course, if he is confirmed in his rank as a marshal and a peer of France, and he proves his worth manfully in those offices, yet nothing can buy him back that one moment that would have made him the master of destiny, if he had been capable of taking it.

That was the terrible revenge taken by the great moment that seldom descends into the life of ordinary mortals, on a man unjustly called upon to seize it who does not know how to exploit it. All the bourgeois virtues of foresight, obedience, zeal and circumspection are helpless, melted down in the fire of a great and fateful moment of destiny that demands nothing less than genius and shapes it into a lasting likeness. Destiny scornfully rejects the hesitant; another god on earth, with fiery arms it raises only the bold into the heaven of heroes.

THE DISCOVERY OF
EL DORADO

J.A. SUTTER, CALIFORNIA

January 1848

A MAN TIRED OF EUROPE

1834. A steamer bound for America is on its way from Le Havre to New York. In the midst of the desperadoes on board, one among hundreds, is John Augustus Sutter, as he will be known, born Johann August Suter in Rynenberg near Basle in Switzerland. Aged thirty-one, he is in a great hurry to put the seven seas between himself and the European law courts. A bankrupt, thief and forger, he has simply abandoned his wife and three children, has got some money together in Paris with the help of a false passport, and is now off in search of a new life. On 7th July he lands in New York, where he spends two years doing all kinds of possible and indeed impossible jobs, becomes a packer, a pharmacist, a dentist, a medicaments salesman and then a tavern-keeper. Finally, having settled to some extent in the city, he buys an inn, settles down in it, sells it again, and following the magic promptings of the time he moves to Missouri. There he sets up as a farmer, within a short time he owns a little property, and he could live a quiet life. But all manner of people keep passing his house—fur traders, hunters, adventurers and soldiers—they are coming from the west and going to the west, and that word "west" gradually acquires a magical sound. First, everyone knows, you come to prairies—prairies with huge herds of buffalo, you can go for days, for weeks on end without seeing a human soul, apart from the Redskins hunting there; then you reach mountains, high and never yet climbed, and then at last that other land of which no one knows anything for certain except that its fabulous wealth is famous: California, still unexplored. A land flowing with milk and honey, free to everyone who wants to take it—but far away, endlessly far away, and mortally dangerous to reach

But John Augustus Sutter has adventurous blood in his veins, and is not tempted to stay put and cultivate the soil on his holding, however good the soil is. One day in 1837 he sells all his possessions, equips an expedition with wagons and horses and herds of buffalo, and sets out from Fort Independence into the unknown.

THE WAY TO CALIFORNIA

1838. Two officers, five missionaries and three women set out in buffalo wagons into the endless void, through prairies and yet more prairies, finally up the mountains and towards the Pacific Ocean. After travelling for three months, they arrive in Fort Vancouver at the end of October. The two officers have left Sutter by then, the missionaries are not going any further, the three women have died of their privations on the way.

Sutter is alone; people try in vain to keep him at Fort Vancouver, offer him a position—he rejects all such suggestions; the lure of the magic name is in his blood.

He begins by crossing the Pacific in a rickety sailing ship to the Sandwich Islands, and after getting into endless difficulties off the coasts of Alaska he lands in a desolate place known as San Francisco. It is not the city of today, which after the earthquake in 1906 has shot up with redoubled growth and has millions of inhabitants—at this time it is a poor fishing village that gets its name from the Franciscan mission; it is not even the capital of the little-known Mexican province of California, lying fallow and desolate without livestock or good growth in the most luxuriant zone of the new continent.

Spanish disorder is made even worse by the absence of any authority, revolts, a shortage of pack animals and human labourers, a shortage of energy to tackle such problems. Sutter hires a horse and takes the animal down into the fertile valley of the Sacramento. A single day is enough to show him that there is not only room for a farm here, indeed for a large estate—there is room for a kingdom. Next day he rides to Monterey, the down-at-heel capital, introduces himself to Governor Alvarado, tells him about his intention of reclaiming the land. He has brought Kanaks with him from the islands, he plans to bring more of those industrious and hard-working indigenous people here regularly; and he takes it upon himself to build settlements and found a small domain called New Helvetia.

"Why New Helvetia?" asks the governor.

"I am a Swiss and a republican," replies Sutter.

"Very well, do as you like. I'll give you a concession for ten years."

Deals, we can conclude, were quickly done there. A thousand miles from any kind of civilization, the energy of a single human being does not carry the same price tag as it does at home.

NEW HELVETIA

1839. A caravan is slowly carting goods along the bank of the Sacramento. Sutter rides ahead on horseback, his gun buckled around him, behind him two or three Europeans, then 150 Kanaks in their short shirts, then thirty buffalo-drawn carts with provisions, seeds and ammunition, fifty horses, seventy-five mules, cows and sheep, then a small rearguard—that is the whole of the army setting out to conquer New Helvetia.

Ahead of them rolls a gigantic wave of fire. They are setting the forests alight as they go along, an easier way of clearing the land than grubbing up the trees. And as soon as the raging flames have swept across the terrain, while the tree stumps are still smoking, they set to work. Storerooms are built, wells dug, seeds sown on soil that needs no ploughing, hurdles are made to pen in the huge flocks and herds. Gradually, more workers arrive from the abandoned mission colonies nearby.

The venture is hugely successful. The seed that has been sown soon yields crops 500 per cent greater than its original quantity. Barns are full to bursting, soon the livestock numbers thousands of animals, and in spite of the local difficulties that are still going on—expeditions against the native inhabitants, who keep making incursions into the flourishing colony—New Helvetia grows to tropically gigantic proportions. Canals are dug, mills and factories built, shipping goes upstream and downstream on the rivers. Sutter supplies not only Fort Vancouver and the Sandwich Islands but also all the ships that put in to the coast of California. He plants fruit, the Californian fruit still so famous and popular today. It does extremely well, so he sends to France and the Rhine for grape vines, and after a few years they cover large areas. He himself builds houses and lays out flourishing farms. He sends to Paris for a piano from the firm of Pleyel—its journey takes 180 days—and to New York for a steam engine, brought right across the continent by sixty buffaloes. He has credits and accounts with the biggest banking houses of England and France, and now, at the age of forty-five, he remembers leaving a wife and three children behind somewhere or other. He writes, inviting them to join him in his principality. For he is aware of all the wealth in his hands: he is the lord of New Helvetia, one of the richest men in the world, and so he intends to remain. At last, moreover, the United States wrests the once-neglected colony from Mexican hands. Now everything is safe and secure. A few more years, and Sutter will be *the* richest man in the world.

A FATEFUL CUT OF THE SPADE

1848, January. James W. Marshall, his carpenter, suddenly comes bursting into John Augustus Sutter's house in a state of great agitation, saying he absolutely must speak to him. Sutter is surprised; only the day before he had sent Marshall up to Coloma and his farm there to begin work on a new sawmill. And now the man has come back without permission, and stands before Sutter quivering with excitement. He makes Sutter go into his office, closes the door and takes from his pocket a handful of sand with a few yellow grains in it. When he was digging yesterday, he says, he noticed this strange metal, and he thought it was gold, but the other men laughed at him. Sutter takes him seriously; he takes the yellow grains, extracts them from the rest of the sand and tests them. Yes, they are gold. He decides to ride up to the farm with Marshall the very next day, but the carpenter is the first to be infected by the terrible fever that will soon be shaking the whole world. He rides back that night in the middle of a storm, impatient for certainty.

Next morning Colonel Sutter is in Coloma himself. They dam the canal and examine the sand. They have only to take a sieve, shake it back and forth for a little while, and the grains of gold are left shining on the black mesh. Sutter assembles the few white men around him, makes them swear on their word of honour to keep quiet about this find until the sawmill is completed. Then he rides back to his farm in a serious and determined mood. He has matters of great import on his mind: as far as anyone can remember gold has never been so easy to pick up, has never lain in the ground so openly, and that ground is his, it is Sutter's property. A decade seems to have passed overnight, and he *is* the richest man in the world.

THE GOLD RUSH

The richest man in the world? No, the poorest, most wretched and disappointed beggar on this earth. After a week the secret is out. A woman—always a woman, of course!—has told some passing stranger and given him a few specks of gold. And there is no precedent for what happens next. All Sutter's men leave their work, the metalworkers leave the smithy, the shepherds and herdsmen leave their flocks and herds, the wine-growers abandon the vines and the soldiers their guns. As if possessed, they all snatch up sieves and pans in haste and run to the sawmill to sift gold from the sand. Overnight the agricultural land has been abandoned, no one milks the dairy cows, who bellow and die miserably, the herds of buffalo tear down their hurdles and stamp through the fields where the crops are rotting on the stalk, no one is making cheese, the barns are in disrepair, the huge clockwork of the vast enterprise has come to a halt. Telegraphy sprinkles the golden promise over land and sea. And already people are arriving from the cities, from the harbours, sailors leave their ships, government officials leave their posts, they are all coming from east and west in long, endless columns, on foot, on horseback or in carts. It is the gold rush, a swarm of human locusts, the gold-diggers. An aimless, brutal horde knowing no law but the law of the fist, no commandment but that of their revolver, pours over the once-flourishing colony. As far as they are concerned no one owns anything here, and no one dares to resist these desperadoes. They slaughter Sutter's cattle, they tear down the barns to build themselves houses, they trample down the crops in his fields, they steal his machinery—overnight John Augustus Sutter is as poor as a beggar. Like King Midas, he is stifled by his own gold.

And this unprecedented storm in search of gold becomes more and more violent; news of it has reached the outside world, 100 ships set off from New York alone, in 1848, 1849,

1850 and 1851 great hordes of adventurers come over from Germany, Great Britain, France and Spain. Some sail round Cape Horn, but that is too long a journey for the most impatient, who take the more dangerous way across the Isthmus of Panama. A company swiftly decides to build a railway line on the isthmus, and thousands of workers die in the fever of its construction just so that the impatient will be saved three or four weeks and they will get at the gold sooner. Huge caravans cross the continent, people of all races and languages, and they all dig up John Augustus Sutter's property as if it were their own. A city rises in dreamlike haste on the site of San Francisco, which belongs to him by virtue of a signed and sealed governmental act, strangers buy and sell his land to and from one another, and the name of New Helvetia, his domain, disappears behind the magic name of El Dorado, California.

Bankrupt again, John Augustus Sutter stares as if dazed at these enormous seeds of discord that have sprung up. First he tries digging with the others, and even with his servants and companions, to exploit the wealth, but everyone leaves him. So he withdraws entirely from the gold-bearing district, to a remote farm near the mountains, away from that accursed river and the wretched sand, to his farm hermitage. At last his wife and their three grown-up children reach him there, but almost as soon as she arrives she dies of the exhaustion of her journey. But he now has three sons, there are eight arms between them, counting his own; and thus equipped John Augustus Sutter sets to work as an agriculturalist. Once again, but now with his sons, he works his way up, a quiet and tough man making use of the fantastic fertility of the soil. Once again he makes a plan, and he keeps it to himself.

THE TRIAL

1850. California has become one of the United States of America. Under the stern rule of the United States, discipline as well as wealth finally come to that part of the country, obsessed as it is with gold. Anarchy is under control, the laws of the land are enforced again.

And now John Augustus Sutter comes forward with his claims. All the land on which the city of San Francisco has been built, he says, is rightfully his. It is the duty of the state, he says, to make amends for all the damage he has suffered by the theft of his property, and he claims his own part of all the gold taken from its soil. A trial begins, of dimensions never before known to mankind. John Augustus Sutter is taking proceedings against 17,221 farmers who have settled in his own plantations, demanding that they vacate the land they have stolen, and he is asking $25 million compensation from the state of California for simply misappropriating the roads, canals, bridges, dams and mills that he built. In addition he wants another $25 million compensation from the United States as a whole for the destruction of his estates, as well as his share of the gold brought out of the ground. He has sent his eldest son, Emil, to study law in Washington so that he can take proper legal action, and he devotes the enormous income from his new farms to the sole purpose of bringing this expensive lawsuit. He takes it through all the courts for four years.

On 15th March 1855 the courts finally decide on a verdict. The incorruptible judge Thompson, who is the highest legal authority in California, recognizes John Augustus Sutter's rights to the land as fully justified and inviolable.

On that day, John Augustus Sutter has achieved his aim, and he is the richest man in the world.

THE END OF THE STORY

The richest man in the world? No, once again the answer is no; he is the poorest and most unfortunate beggar in the world, he is a broken man. When news of the verdict arrives a storm breaks out in San Francisco and its surroundings. Tens of thousands band together, all the people who think they own property but are now under threat, a streetwise mob, a rabble that delights in looting. They break into the Hall of Justice and burn it down, they go in search of the judge, meaning to lynch him, and they set off in a vast throng to plunder all John Augustus Sutter's property. His eldest son, threatened by these bandits, shoots himself; his second son is murdered; the third runs for it but is drowned on the way home. A wave of fire sweeps over New Helvetia, Sutter's farms burn down, his vineyards are trampled underfoot, his furniture, collections and money are stolen and his entire vast property laid waste with pitiless fury. Sutter himself only just escapes with his life.

John Augustus Sutter never recovers from this blow. His work has been destroyed, his wife and children are dead, his mind is confused. Only one idea still flickers faintly in his now-stupefied brain: the law laid down at the trial.

For twenty-five years an old, feeble-minded and poorly dressed man still haunts the Hall of Justice in Washington. The "general" in his grubby overcoat and well-worn shoes, demanding the restitution of his billions, is a familiar figure in all the offices there. And there are always advocates, adventurers and crooks to be found ready to get the last of his pension out of him by persuading him to go to law again. Himself, he does not want money; he hates the gold that has made him poor, has killed his three children and wrecked his life. All he wants is justice, and he defends himself with the querulous embitterment of a monomaniac. He complains to the Senate, he complains to Congress, he puts his trust in all kinds of helpers who, going about the business in just the wrong way, put a ridiculous military uniform on him and drag the unfortunate man as their puppet from office to office, from one set of deputies to another. This goes on for twenty years, from 1860 to 1880, twenty wretched years of beggary. Day after day he wanders around the Capitol, a laughing stock to all the civil servants, mocked by the street urchins—he who owns the richest land on earth, and on whose property the second capital of the gigantic country stands, growing hourly. However, he is left awkwardly waiting. And there, on the steps of Congress, the heart attack that comes as a release strikes him down on the afternoon of 17th June 1880—and a beggar is carried away, dead. A dead beggar, but one with a polemical treatise in his pocket ensuring a claim to the greatest fortune in history to him and his heirs.

No one has ever claimed Sutter's inheritance, no descendant has come forward. San Francisco and all the land around stands on a stranger's property. No one has ever stated the rights of the case, and only one writer, Blaise Cendrars, has at least given John Augustus Sutter what is due to a great fate: the right to be remembered by posterity with admiration.

THE FIRST WORD TO CROSS THE OCEAN

―――

CYRUS W. FIELD

―――

28 July 1858

THE NEW RHYTHM

For all the thousands, perhaps hundreds of thousands of years since that strange being known as man has walked the earth, there has been no other maximum degree of human movement than the pace of a horse, of a wheel going round, or of a ship propelled by oars or sails. All the wealth of technical progress within that narrow area illuminated by consciousness that we call the history of the world had yielded no noticeable acceleration in the rhythm of movement. Wallenstein's armies advanced hardly any faster than Caesar's legions; Napoleon's troops were no swifter than the hordes of Genghis Khan; Nelson's corvettes crossed the sea only a little faster than the pirate ships of Viking raiders and Phoenician trading vessels. Lord Byron on his journey as Childe Harold covers no more miles a day than Ovid on his way to exile in Pontus; in the eighteenth century Goethe does not travel in conspicuously more comfort or at greater speed than the Apostle Paul at the beginning of the millennium. Countries lie the same distance from each other in time and space in the age of Napoleon and under the Roman Empire; the resistance of matter still triumphs over the human will.

Only the nineteenth century brings fundamental change to the extent and rhythm of terrestrial speed. In its first and second decades, nations and countries come together faster than for millennia before them. Railways and steamers enable people to cover what were once journeys of many days in a single day, previously endless hours of travel can be completed in time measured by quarters of an hour and minutes. But however much the triumphant new speeds achieved by trains and steamboats are appreciated by contemporaries, such inventions still lie within the sphere of what the mind can grasp. For all these vehicles do, after all, is to multiply previously known speeds five, ten, twenty times over; the outward sight and inner meaning of them can still be followed, and what looks miraculous can be explained. However, the first achievements of electricity, a Hercules still in the cradle, appear entirely unexpected, overturning all earlier laws, smashing all current dimensions. We who were born later will never feel the amazement of that generation faced with the first feats of the electric telegraph, the vast and enthusiastic astonishment on seeing the same small, barely perceptible electric spark—yesterday only just capable of crackling an inch up from a Leiden jar to the knuckle of your finger—suddenly gaining the demonic power to leap across countries, mountains, whole parts of this earth. Or grasping the idea, scarcely thought out yet to its end, that when the ink is still wet on a written word it can be received thousands of miles away in the same second, can be read and understood, and that the invisible current swinging between the two poles of the tiny voltaic pile can be stretched over the whole earth from one end to the other. Or the thought that the apparatus of the physics laboratory, apparently toy-like, that yesterday was just capable of attracting a few shreds of paper if you rubbed a glass plate, can acquire the power of human muscular strength and speed multiplied by millions and billions, carrying messages, moving railway trains, filling streets and buildings with light, and like Ariel hovering invisibly through the air. Only this discovery brought the most crucial readjustment since the creation of the world to the relationship of space and time.

The year 1837—of such significance to the world, when the telegraph made it possible for previously isolated human experiences to be felt simultaneously—is seldom even mentioned in school textbooks, which unfortunately still think it more important to write about the wars and victories of individual nations and military commanders than what are the true triumphs of mankind, because they were achieved jointly. Yet no other date in recent history can be compared with it for the psychological effect of this readjustment of the value of time. The world has changed since it became possible to be in Paris and know simultaneously what is going on in Amsterdam, Moscow, Naples and Lisbon at that very minute. Only one last step has yet to be taken, and then the other parts of the world will also be included in that great connection and a common consciousness of all mankind will be created.

But nature still resists this last unification, still comes up against an obstacle. For another two decades all those countries cut off from each other by the sea will be separated. For a while, thanks to the insulating properties of porcelain, the spark can spring along telegraph poles unimpeded, water sucks up the electric current. But electric wiring cannot be laid through the sea until a means of entirely insulating copper and iron wires has been discovered.

In times of progress, luckily, one invention lends a helping hand to another. A few years after the introduction of telegraph lines on land, gutta-percha is found to be a suitable material for insulating electric cables in water. Now a start can be made on connecting the most important country outside the continent of Europe, Great Britain, to the European telegraph network. An engineer called Brett lays the first cable at the same place where Blériot, later, will be the first to cross the Channel in an airplane. A ridiculous incident intervenes to prevent immediate success: a fisherman in Boulogne, thinking he has found a particularly fat eel, tears the cable out after it has been laid. But on 13th November 1851, the second attempt does succeed. Great Britain is now connected to the Continent, and thus Europe truly becomes Europe, a being that experiences all that is happening with a single brain and a single heart at the same time.

Such a huge success within so few years—for what does a decade mean in the history of mankind?—must naturally arouse boundless courage in the generation that knows it. Everything that you try succeeds, and at dreamlike speed. Only a few years, and Great Britain in turn is connected by telegraph with Ireland, Denmark with Sweden and Corsica with the mainland, and attempts are already being made to connect Egypt and India to the network. One part of the world, however—the most important part—seems doomed to perpetual exclusion from the chain that spans the rest of the world: America. For how can the Atlantic or Pacific Ocean, neither of which has anywhere to stop in its endless breadth, be crossed by a single wire? All factors are still unknown in the infancy of electricity. The depth of the sea has not been plumbed yet, there is only a vague idea of the geological structure of the ocean, and no one has discovered whether a wire laid so deep could stand up to the pressure of so much water above it. And even if it were technically possible to embed so long a cable safely at such depths, where can a ship be found large enough to carry the weight of 2,000 miles of iron and copper cable? Or dynamos powerful enough to send an unbroken electric current over a distance that a steamer would take at least two to three weeks to cross? People of that time lack any relevant assumptions. No one yet knows whether magnetic currents that could divert the electric current circle in the depths of the ocean, no one has good enough insulation, proper measuring apparatus; all that is known so far is the first laws of electricity that have just opened human eyes from their centuries of sleep in oblivion. "Impossible! Absurd!" say scholars, vigorously rejecting the idea as soon as anyone even mentions a plan for telegraphy to span the ocean. "Later, maybe," say the boldest of the technical experts. Such a plan seems a daring exploit with an incalculable outcome even to Morse, the man to whom the electric telegraph owes its greatest perfection so far. But he adds, prophetically, that if the exploit were to succeed, the laying of the transatlantic cable would be regarded as "the great feat of the century".

For a miracle or something miraculous to be perfected, the first step is always the faith of an individual in that miracle. The naïve courage of someone whose mind is closed to reason may give a creative impulse where the learned hesitate to tread, and here, as usual, a simple coincidence sets the grandiose undertaking going. In the year 1854 an English engineer by the name of Gisborne, who wants to lay a cable from New York to the easternmost point of America, Newfoundland, so that news from the ships can be received a few days earlier, has to stop in the middle of his work when his funds run out. So he goes to New York in search of someone to finance him, and there, by pure chance—the father of so many famous things—he meets a young man called Cyrus W. Field, son of a clergyman, who has done so well and so quickly in business that even at a youthful age he could retire to private life with a large fortune if he wanted. At present he follows no profession, but he is too young and too energetic for inactivity in the long run, and Gisborne seeks him out to arouse his interest in laying the cable from New York to Newfoundland. Cyrus W. Field is not—it is tempting to say that luckily he is not—a technologist or any kind of expert. He knows nothing about electricity, he has never seen a cable. But there is a passionate belief in this clergyman's son, the energetic audacity typical of an American. Where the professional engineer Gisborne sees only the immediate aim of connecting New York to Newfoundland, the young enthusiast immediately looks further ahead. Why not connect Newfoundland to Ireland by a cable under the sea next? With an energy determined to overcome all obstacles—he crossed the Atlantic both ways thirty-one times in those years—Cyrus W. Field sets to work at once, firmly intent upon devoting everything in and around him to his purpose, thereby igniting the idea, thanks to which its explosive force becomes reality. The new, wonderful power of electricity has thus allied itself to the other strongest dynamic element of life: the human will. A man has found his life's work, and a task has found the man to carry it out.

PREPARATION

Cyrus W. Field begins his work with improbable energy. He gets in touch with all the professionals, besieges governments with requests for concessions, leads a campaign in both parts of the world to raise the necessary funds; and so forceful is this entirely unknown man, so impassioned his personal conviction, so powerful his belief in electricity as a new miraculous force, that the equity capital of £350,000 was fully subscribed in Great Britain within a few days. Once the richest businessmen of Liverpool, Manchester and London have come together to found the Telegraph Construction and Maintenance Company, the money streams in. However, the subscribers also include such names as those of Thackeray and Lady Byron, who have no secondary business aim in mind and want to support the work purely out of moral enthusiasm; nothing illustrates the optimistic attitude towards everything technical and mechanical that animated Great Britain in the age of Stephenson, Brunel and the other great engineers as well as the fact that a single appeal is enough to raise such an enormous sum of money for an entirely fantastic venture, from subscribers who cannot be guaranteed that they will recover their investment.

For the enormous expense of laying the cable is all that can be reliably calculated at the beginning of the enterprise.

There is no model for the actual technical method of carrying it out. In the nineteenth century, nothing of similar dimensions had ever been devised or planned before. How could spanning an entire ocean be compared with bridging the narrow strip of water between Dover and Calais? There, it had been enough to reel out thirty or forty miles of cable from the deck of an ordinary paddle steamer, and it unwound as easily as an anchor from its winch. And for laying a cable in the English Channel, you could wait for a particularly calm day, you knew the precise depth of the seabed, you were always within sight of one shore or the other and thus not in any danger; the connection could be made comfortably within a single day. But during an ocean crossing of at least three weeks constantly at sea, a reel of cable a hundred times longer and heavier cannot stay exposed on deck to all the rigours of the weather. Furthermore, no ship of the time is large enough to carry that gigantic cocoon of iron, copper and gutta-percha in its hold, or strong enough to carry such a load. Two ships at least will be needed, and these main ships must in turn be accompanied by others so that they can keep precisely to the shortest course and have help ready to hand in the case of any accident. It is true that the British government has made the *Agamemnon* available for this venture—one of its largest warships, a vessel that fought off Sebastopol—and the American government had contributed the *Niagara*, a frigate of 5,000 tons, the largest possible at the time. However, both ships must be specially converted first, so that each can carry half of the endless chain intended to link two parts of the world with each other. But the main problem remains the cable itself. That gigantic umbilical cord between two parts of this earth is exposed to unimaginable stress. For one thing, the cable must be as strong and resistant as a steel rope, and at the same time elastic enough to be easily paid out. It must stand up to any pressure and any strain, and yet be as easy to tie off smoothly as a silk thread. It must be massive, yet not take up too much space; it must be solid, yet sensitive enough to let the slightest electric wave pass along it for 2,000 miles. The smallest tear in it, the least unevenness at any single part of this gigantic cable can wreck it on its fourteen-day journey.

But the venture is made. Factories are at work day and night, all the cogwheels drive that one man's demonic will forward. Whole mines of iron and copper are needed for this one cable, whole forests of rubber trees must be tapped to make the gutta-percha insulation to cover such a great distance. And nothing more vividly illustrates the enormous proportions of the enterprise than the fact that 367,000 miles of a single wire are spun into this one cable, thirteen times as much as would go around the entire earth, and enough to connect the earth with the moon in a single line. Not since the building of the Tower of Babel has mankind ventured anything more technically magnificent.

THE FIRST START

The machinery whirrs for a year, wire reels out from the factories into both ships all the time like a thin, flowing thread, and at last, after thousands and thousands of revolutions, half the cable is rolled up in a spool on each of the ships. The new, cumbersome engines have also been built and installed; provided with brakes and a reverse gear, they are to lower the cable to the depths of the ocean in an uninterrupted process taking one, two or three weeks. The best electricians and technical experts, including Morse himself, have assembled on board in order to keep an eye on their apparatus and check it while the cable is being laid to make sure that there is no break in the electric current. Reporters and artists have joined the fleet as well to describe this voyage, the most exciting since the days of Columbus and Magellan in words and pictures.

At last everything is ready for the ships to leave, and although hitherto sceptics have been in the majority, the public interest of Great Britain as a whole now turns to passionate enthusiasm for the venture. On 5th August 1857, hundreds of small boats and ships are circling around the fleet carrying the cable in the little Irish harbour of Valentia to take part in the historic moment when one end of the cable is carried to the coast by boats and made fast on the mainland of Europe. The departure of the ships becomes a solemn occasion. The government has sent representatives, and in a moving address a priest prays for God's blessing on the bold venture. "O Eternal God," he begins, "Thou who hast spread out the heavens and mastered the surging of the sea, Thou whom the winds and the waves obey, in Thy mercy look down on Thy servants... hold sway over every obstacle, remove all resistance that might prevent us from carrying out the performance of this great work." And then thousands of hands wave and thousands of hats are raised from the shore and the sea. Slowly, the land disappears. An attempt is being made to realize one of mankind's boldest dreams.

A MISFORTUNE

The original plan had been for the two great ships, the *Agamemnon* and the *Niagara*, each carrying half the cable, to arrive with each other at a point in the middle of the ocean, calculated in advance, and only there would the two halves be riveted together. Then one ship was to steer west for Newfoundland, the other east to Ireland. But it seemed too audacious to venture so much expensive cable at the first attempt, so it was decided, instead, to lay the first part of the line from the mainland while no one yet knew for certain whether telegraphic transmission beneath the sea worked properly at all over such distances.

Of the two vessels, the task of laying the cable from the mainland to the middle of the sea is given to the *Niagara*. Slowly and cautiously, the American frigate steers a course to that point, all the time leaving the thread of the cable behind like a spider spinning silk from its huge body. Slowly and regularly, the engine laying the cable rattles on board the ship—it is the sound well known to all seamen of an anchor cable being paid out as it unreels from the winch. After a few hours the men on board pay no more attention to the regular grinding sound than they do to their own heartbeats.

Further and further out to sea, always lowering the cable into the water behind the keel. This adventure seems far from adventurous. Only the electricians sit in a special room listening, constantly exchanging signals with the Irish mainland. And, wonderful to relate, although the coast has long ago been out of sight, transmission along the underwater cable is as clear as if one European city were communicating with another. They have already left the shallow waters behind, they are part of the way over what is known as the deep-sea plateau that rises beyond Ireland, and still the metal thread is running regularly down behind the keel like sand in an hourglass, sending and receiving messages at the same time.

Three hundred and thirty-five miles of cable have already been laid, more than ten times the distance from Dover to Calais; five days and five nights of initial uncertainty have already passed, and on the sixth evening, on 11th August, Cyrus W. Field is going to bed after many hours of work and stress to get some well-earned rest. Then, suddenly—what has happened?—the rattling sound stops. And just as someone sleeping in a moving train starts up when the locomotive unexpectedly stops, just as the miller wakes in his bed when the mill-wheel suddenly stops going round, so all on board the ship are instantly awake and running up on deck. A first glance at the engine shows that the reel running out is empty. The cable has suddenly slipped off the winch, it was impossible to catch the end that came away in time, and now it is even more impossible to find the lost end in the depths and bring it up again. A terrible thing has happened. A small technical fault has wrecked the work of years. The men who set out so boldly return, defeated, to Great Britain, where the sudden silencing of all signals has already paved the way for bad news.

MISFORTUNE AGAIN

Cyrus Field, the only imperturbable man involved, hero and businessman both, takes stock. What has been lost? Three hundred miles of cable, £100,000 of share capital, and—what troubles him even more—a whole irreplaceable year. For the expedition can hope for good weather only in summer, and this year the season is already too far advanced to try again. On the other side of the account that Field is drawing up, there is a small profit: a great deal of practical experience has been gained in this first attempt. The cable itself, having proved its worth, can be wound up and put away ready for the next expedition. Only the engines for laying the cable, which were to blame for the fateful break in it, must be altered.

So another year passes in waiting and preparatory work. Not until 10th June 1858 can the same ships set out again, with a cargo of new courage and the old cable. As the electrical transmission of signals worked perfectly on the first voyage, Field and the others have returned to the old plan of beginning to lay cables out on both sides from the middle of the ocean. The first few days of the second voyage pass without incident. Only on the seventh day is the laying of the cable, and thus the real work, to begin at the place calculated in advance. Up to this point everything is, or seems to be, a pleasure cruise. The engines are not in use, the sailors can rest and enjoy the fine weather, the sky is cloudless and the water still—perhaps too still.

On the third day, however, the captain of the *Agamemnon* feels secretly uneasy. A glance at the barometer has shown him how alarmingly fast the quicksilver column is falling. A storm of an unusual kind must be brewing, and sure enough a storm does break on the fourth day, such a storm as even the most experienced seamen on the Atlantic Ocean have seldom seen. This hurricane strikes the British cable-laying ship, the *Agamemnon*, with fatal severity. In itself an excellent vessel that has withstood the harshest trials in all seas and even in war, the flagship of the British Navy ought to be able to withstand this terrible storm as well. But unfortunately the ship has been entirely converted for laying the cables in order to accommodate such a huge weight. This is not like a freighter, where the weight can be equally distributed on all sides of the hold; the whole weight of the gigantic spool lies in the middle, and only part of it is entirely in the foreship, with the even worse result that every time the ship goes up and down in rough seas that part of the ship swings back and forth with redoubled force. That means that the storm can play a dangerous game with its victim: the ship is raised forward and backward up to an angle of forty-five degrees, breakers flood down on the deck, any objects not lashed down there are smashed. Then there is another misfortune—in the worst of the storm, when the ship is shaken from the keel to the mast, the shed containing the cargo of coal heaped on deck gives way. The whole mass comes down like a storm of black hail over the sailors, who are already bleeding and exhausted. Some are injured by their fall, others scalded as pans tip over in the galley. One sailor goes mad in the ten-day storm, and the crew are already thinking of the desperate measure of throwing part of the fateful cable overboard. Fortunately the captain refuses to take the responsibility for that, and he is right. The *Agamemnon* survives the ten days of storm, after unspeakable travails, and although badly delayed manages to join the other vessels at the place in the ocean where the laying of the cable was to begin.

Only now, however, is it clear how much the valuable and sensitive cargo of wires has suffered, entangled thousands of times as it was flung back and forth in heavy seas. The separate wires are intertwined in many places, their gutta-percha covering is rubbed or torn. Without much confidence, they make a few attempts to lay the cable all the same, but the only result is the loss of some 200 miles of cable that disappear uselessly into the sea. For the second time the voyage has to be abandoned, and they go home, not in triumph but crestfallen.

THE THIRD VOYAGE

Pale-faced and already aware of the bad news, the shareholders in London are waiting for their leader—and the man who tempted them into the venture—Cyrus W. Field. Half of the share capital has been lost on those two voyages, and nothing has been proved, nothing achieved. It is understandable that most of them now feel enough has been done. The chairman advises salvaging what can still be salvaged. He is in favour of bringing what remains of the cable back from the ships and selling it, if necessary even at a loss, before drawing a line under that wild plan to stretch a telegraph line under the ocean. The deputy chairman closes ranks with him and sends notice of his resignation in writing, to demonstrate that he wants no more to do with the absurd enterprise. But there is no shaking the tenacity and idealism of Cyrus W. Field. Nothing is lost, he explains. The cable itself passed the test with flying colours, and there is still enough on board to make a new attempt; the fleet is assembled, the crews hired. The very fact that there was such an unusual storm last time suggests that the ships can hope for a period of fine, calm weather now. Courage, he says, take heart again! Now or never is the opportunity to dare the ultimate venture.

The shareholders look at one another more and more uncertainly: are they to entrust the last of the capital they paid into the scheme to this fool? But as a strong will will always finally sweep the hesitant away with it, Cyrus W. Field forces the others to decide on another voyage. On 17th July 1858, five weeks after the last, disastrous voyage, the fleet leaves its British harbour for the third time.

And now the truth of the old adage that crucial matters almost always succeed in secret is confirmed. This time there are no observers of the departure; no boats large or small circle round the ships wishing them luck, no crowd gathers on the beach, no festive dinner is held, no speech is made, no priest calls on God to be with the enterprise. The ships put out to sea, surreptitiously and in silence. But a kindly sea awaits them. Precisely on the day agreed, 28th July, eleven days after the departure from Queenstown, the *Agamemnon* and the *Niagara* are able to begin their great task at the appointed place in the middle of the ocean.

THE FIRST WORD TO CROSS THE OCEAN

It is a strange sight. The ships turn to each other, stern to stern. The ends of the cable are riveted together between them. Without any formality—and even the men on board, tired as they are of unsuccessful attempts, watch with little interest—the iron and copper cable sinks down between the two ships to the bottom of the sea, unplumbed as yet by any lead-line. There is one more greeting from deck to deck, flag to flag, and the British ship steers for Britain, the American ship for America. While they move away from each other, two wandering points in the endless ocean, the cable constantly holds them together—and for the first time in human history two ships can communicate with each other beyond wind and water, space and distance, now invisible to one another. Every few hours one of the vessels sends an electric signal from the depths of the ocean recording the number of miles it has travelled, and every time the other ship confirms that, thanks to the good weather, she too has gone the same distance. A day passes like this, and then another, a third, a fourth. At last, on 5th August, the *Niagara* is able to report its arrival in Trinity Bay, Newfoundland, and can see the American coast ahead, after laying no less than 1,030 miles of cable. The *Agamemnon* is likewise triumphant, having also embedded about 1,000 miles securely in the depths, and the British ship has the Irish coast in sight. But only those two ships, those few hundred men in their wooden accommodation, know that the deed has been done. The world is not aware of it yet, having forgotten the venture long ago. No one is waiting for them on the beach in Newfoundland or Ireland—but in that single second when the new cable under the ocean joins the cable on land, the whole of mankind will know of their great joint victory.

THE GREAT HOSANNA

It is for the very reason that this lightning flash of joy strikes out of a clear blue sky that it burns so brightly. The old and the new continents receive news of the project's success at almost the same hour early in August. The effect is indescribable. *The Times*, usually thoughtful and measured in its pronouncements, says in a leading article: "Since the discovery of Columbus, nothing has been done in any degree comparable to the vast enlargement which has thus been given to the sphere of human activity." The City is in a state of great excitement. But the pride and delight felt in Great Britain is restrained and muted by comparison with the hurricane of enthusiasm in America as soon as the news breaks there. Business grinds to a halt, the streets are crowded with people asking questions and deep in loud discussion. A complete unknown, Cyrus W. Field, has become the hero of an entire nation overnight. He is placed firmly beside Franklin and Columbus; the whole of New York and a hundred more cities are agog with expectation to see the man whose determination has brought about "the marriage of young America and the Old World". But the enthusiasm has not yet reached its highest point; for the time being, there is nothing to go on but the dry announcement that the cable has been laid. However, can it speak as well? Has the achievement really succeeded? It is a great spectacle—an entire city, an entire country is waiting and listening for a single word, the first word to cross the ocean. Everyone knows that the Queen of England will be first to send a message of congratulation, and it is expected ever more impatiently hour by hour. But days and days pass, because by unlucky chance the cable to Newfoundland has been destroyed, and it is not until 16th August that the message from Queen Victoria reaches New York in the evening.

The much-desired news arrives too late for the papers to print the official information; only a summary can be delivered to the telegraph and newspaper offices, and at once huge crowds gather. Newspaper boys have to make their way through the turmoil dishevelled, their clothes torn. The news is announced in the city's restaurants and theatres. Thousands who cannot yet grasp the fact that a telegraph message can arrive many days ahead of the fastest ship run down to the harbour in Brooklyn to welcome the heroic ship responsible for this peaceful victory, the *Niagara*. Next day, 17th August, the newspapers rejoice in headlines as thick as a finger: "The cable in perfect working order", "Everybody crazy with joy", "Tremendous sensation throughout the city", "Now's the time for an universal jubilee". It is an unheard-of sensation: for the first time since thinking began on earth, a thought has crossed the ocean in the time it took to think it. And already 100 cannon shots are thundering out from the Battery to announce that the President of the United States has replied to the Queen. No one dares to doubt now; that evening New York and all the other cities are radiant with tens of thousands of lights and torches. Every window is illuminated, and the fact that the dome of City Hall burns down hardly disturbs the joyful celebrations. For the very next day brings new rejoicings: the *Niagara* has arrived; the great hero Cyrus W. Field is there! The rest of the cable is carried through the city in triumph, and the ship's crew is fêted. Such manifestations are repeated daily in every city from the Pacific Ocean to the Gulf of Mexico, as if America were celebrating its discovery for the second time.

Yet still that is not enough! The real triumphal procession is to be even more ostentatious, the finest the New World has ever seen. The preparations take two weeks, and then, on 31st August, a whole city celebrates the work of a single man, Cyrus W. Field, as hardly any victor since the days of the Caesars and the emperors has ever been applauded by his people. A festive procession is made ready on that fine autumn day, so long a procession that it takes six hours to go from one end of the city to the other. Regiments march ahead with banners through streets lined by flags, followed in an endless line by wind bands, singing groups and societies, the fire brigade, the schools and the veterans. Everyone who can march does, everyone who can sing does, everyone who can rejoice rejoices. Cyrus W. Field is driven through the city in a carriage and four, like an emperor of antiquity celebrating his triumph, with the captain of the *Niagara* in another and the President of the United States in a third, with the mayor, the officials and the professors following behind. There are endless speeches, banquets, torchlight processions, the church bells peal, the cannon thunder, and again and again rejoicing surrounds the new Columbus who has united the two worlds, the conqueror of space, the man who in this hour has become the most famous and idolized man in America, Cyrus W. Field.

CRUCIFY HIM!

Thousands, millions of voices are shouting in jubilation that day. Only one voice, the most important, remains strangely silent during the celebrations—the voice of the electric telegraph. In the midst of the rejoicing, perhaps Cyrus W. Field guesses the terrible truth, and it must have been appalling for him to be the only one who knew that on that very day the Atlantic cable has stopped working after, in the last few days, increasingly confused and barely legible signals had come in. Finally the wire has drawn its last, dying breath. In all America no one knows or guesses at the gradual failure, apart from the few who control the reception of transmissions in Newfoundland, and even they, in view of the unbounded rejoicing, hesitate for several days to pass on the bitter information to the jubilant crowds. Soon, however, people begin to notice the paucity of incoming messages. America had expected that now news would be flashing over the ocean every hour—instead, there is only, from time to time, a vague announcement that cannot be checked. It is not long before a rumour is being whispered: in enthusiasm and impatience to achieve better transmissions, over-strong electrical charges have been sent along the line, thus entirely wrecking the cable that was inadequate anyway. They still hope to put things right, but soon there is no denying that the signals are getting more indistinct and less and less comprehensible. Just after that wretched morning following the festivities, on 1st September, clear tones and distinct vibrations stop crossing the sea entirely.

There is nothing that human beings are less likely to forgive than being brought down to earth in the middle of genuinely felt enthusiasm, and seeing themselves disappointed behind their backs by a man of whom they expect everything. As soon as the rumour that the much-famed telegraph has failed is proved true, the stormy current of jubilation turns to a reverse wave of vicious embitterment breaking over Cyrus W. Field, the innocently guilty party. He has deceived a city, a country, the whole world; they are saying in the City of London that he knew about the failure of the telegraph long before it happened, but selfishly let himself enjoy the adulation while he used the time to sell his own shares at a huge profit. There are even more vicious accusations, including the strangest of all, the peremptory claim that the Atlantic telegraph never worked properly; everything said about it was deception and humbug, and the telegram from Queen Victoria had been written in advance and never came over the oceanic telegraph line. Not a single message, says this rumour, really came across the seas in comprehensible form all that time, and the directors of the company simply thought up imaginary messages consisting of assumptions and fragmentary signals. A positive scandal breaks out. Those who were most jubilant yesterday are the most indignant now. An entire city, an entire country is ashamed of its overheated and over-hasty enthusiasm. Cyrus W. Field becomes the victim of this fury; only yesterday still a national hero, regarded as the brother of Franklin and in the line of descent from Columbus, he has to hide like a malefactor from his former friends and admirers. A single day made his fame, a single day has destroyed it. The ill effects cannot be foreseen, the capital is lost, confidence is gone; and, like the legendary serpent of Midgard, the useless cable lies in the unseen depths of the ocean.

SIX YEARS OF SILENCE

The forgotten cable lies useless in the ocean for six years; for six years the old, cold silence lords it once again over the two continents that, for a brief time, sent pulsating signals to each other. Two continents that had been as close as a breath once drawn, as close as a few hundred words, America and Europe are separated, as they have been for millennia, by insuperable distance. The boldest plan of the nineteenth century, only yesterday almost reality, has become a legend once more, a myth. Of course no one thinks of returning to the project that half succeeded; the terrible defeat has crippled all their powers and stifled all their enthusiasm. In America the civil war between the north and the south diverts all attention from other questions; in Great Britain committees still meet now and then, but it takes them two years to come to the arid conclusion that, in principle, a cable running under the sea would be possible. But the path from academic theory to application of the principle is not one that anyone thinks of treading. For six years, all work on the project lies as much at rest as the forgotten cable at the bottom of the sea.

However, while six years are only a fleeting moment within the huge space of history, they mean as much as a thousand in so young a science as electricity. Every year, every month brings new discoveries in that field. Dynamos become stronger and stronger, more and more precise, have more and more applications, the functioning of electrical apparatus is ever more exact. The telegraph network already spans the internal areas of all the continents; it has already crossed the Mediterranean and linked Africa and Europe. So as year follows year the idea of crossing the Atlantic Ocean imperceptibly comes to lose more and more of the fantastic aura that has clung to it for so long. The time when the attempt is made again is bound to come inexorably closer. All that is missing is the man to infuse new energy into the old plan.

And suddenly the man is there—and lo and behold, he is the same man as before, with the same faith and confidence in the idea: Cyrus W. Field, resurrected from the exile of silence and malicious scorn. He has crossed the ocean for the thirtieth time and returns to London; he succeeds in providing new capital of £600,000 for the old concessions. And at last the giant ship he has dreamt of so long is also available, a vessel that can carry the enormous freight on its own, the famous *Great Eastern*, with its 22,000 tons and four funnels, built by Isambard Kingdom Brunel. Furthermore, wonderful to relate, it is not in use this year because, like the undersea cable project itself, it is ahead of its time. It can be bought and equipped for the expedition within two days.

Now everything that was once immeasurably difficult is easy. The mammoth ship, carrying a new cable, leaves the Thames on 23rd July 1865. Although the first attempt fails because of a tear in the cable two days before the laying is completed, and the insatiable ocean swallows up £600,000 sterling, technology is now too sure of itself to be discouraged. And when the *Great Eastern* sets out for the second time on 13th July 1866, the voyage is a triumph. This time the cable calls back to Europe clearly and distinctly. A few days later the old, lost cable is found, and two strands of cable now link the Old and New Worlds into one. What was miraculous yesterday is taken for granted today, and from that moment on the earth has, so to speak, a single heartbeat. Mankind now lives able to hear, see and understand itself simultaneously from one end of the earth to the other, made divinely omnipresent by its own creative power. And, thanks to its victory over space and time, mankind would be united for ever, if it were not confused again and again by the fateful delusion constantly destroying that grandiose union, enabling it to destroy itself by the same means that give it power over the elements.

THE RACE TO REACH
THE SOUTH POLE

CAPTAIN SCOTT,
90 DEGREES LATITUDE

16 January 1912

THE STRUGGLE FOR THE EARTH

The twentieth century looks down on a world without mysteries. All its countries have been explored, ships have ploughed their way through the most distant seas. Landscapes that only a generation ago still slumbered in blissful anonymity serve the needs of Europe; steamers go as far as the long-sought sources of the Nile. The Victoria Falls, first seen by a European only half a century ago, obediently generate electricity; the Amazon rainforest, that last wilderness, has been cleared; the frontiers of Tibet, the only country that was still virgin territory, have been breached. New drawing by knowledgeable hands now covers the words *Terra incognita* on old maps and globes; in the twentieth century, mankind knows the planet on which it lives. Already the enquiring will is looking for new paths; it must plunge down to the fantastic fauna of the deep sea, or soar up into the endless air. For untrodden paths are to be found only in the skies, and already the steel swallows of aeroplanes shoot up, racing each other, to reach new heights and new distances, now that the earth lies fallow and can reveal no more secrets to human curiosity.

But one final secret preserved the earth's modesty from our gaze into the present century, two tiny parts of its racked and tormented body were still saved from the greed of its own inhabitants: the South Pole and the North Pole, its backbone, two places with almost no character or meaning in themselves, around which its axis has been turning for thousands of years. The earth has protected them, leaving them pure and spotless. It has placed barriers of ice in front of this last mystery, setting eternal winter to guard them against the greedy. Access is forbidden by imperious frost and storms; danger and terror scare away the bold with the menace of death. No human eyes may dwell on this closed sphere, and even the sun takes only a fleeting glance.

Expeditions have followed one another for decades. None has achieved its aim. The body of the boldest of the bold, Andrée, who hoped to fly over the Pole in a balloon and never returned, has rested in the glass coffin of the ice for thirty-three years and has only now been discovered. Every attempt is dashed to pieces on the sheer walls of frost. The earth has hidden her face here for thousands of years, up to our own day, triumphing for the last time over the will of her own creatures. Her modesty, pure and virginal, defies the curiosity of the world.

But the young twentieth century reaches out its hands impatiently. It has forged new weapons in laboratories, found new ways to arm itself against danger, and all resistance only increases its avidity. It wants to know the whole truth, in its very first decade it aims to conquer what all the millennia before could not. The rivalry of nations keeps company with the courage of individuals. They are not competing only to reach the Pole now, but also for the honour of flying the national flag first over newly discovered land: it is a crusade of races and nations against places hallowed by longing. The onslaught is renewed from all quarters of the earth. Mankind waits impatiently, knowing that the prize is the last secret of the place where we live. Peary and Cook prepare to set out from America to conquer the North Pole, while two ships steer southward, one commanded by the Norwegian explorer Amundsen, the other by an Englishman, Captain Scott.

SCOTT

Scott, a captain in the British Navy. An average captain, with a record befitting his rank behind him. He has served to the satisfaction of his superior officers, and later took part in Shackleton's expedition. Nothing in his conduct suggests that he is a hero. His face, reflected by photography, could be that of 1,000 Englishmen, 10,000: cold, energetic, showing no play of muscles, as if frozen hard by interior energy. His eyes are steely grey, his mouth firmly closed. Not a romantic line in it anywhere, not a gleam of humour in a countenance made up of will-power and practical knowledge of the world. His handwriting is any Englishman's handwriting, no shading or flourishes, swift and sure. His style is clear and correct, strikingly factual, yet as unimaginative as a report. Scott writes English as Tacitus writes Latin, as if carving it in unhewn stone. You sense that he is a man who does not dream, fanatically objective, in fact a true blue Englishman in whom even genius takes the crystalline form of a pronounced sense of duty. Men like Scott have featured hundreds of times in British history, conquering India and nameless islands in the East Indian archipelago, colonizing Africa and fighting battles against the whole world, always with the same iron energy, the same collective consciousness and the same cold, reserved expression.

But his will is hard as steel; you can sense that before he takes any action. Scott intends to finish what Shackleton began. He equips an expedition, but his financial means are inadequate. That does not deter him. He sacrifices his own fortune and runs up debts in the certainty of success. His young wife bears him a son, but like another Hector he does not hesitate to leave his Andromache. He soon finds friends and companions; nothing on earth can change his mind now. The strange ship that is to take the expedition to the edge of the Antarctic Ocean is called the *Terra Nova*—strange because it has two kinds of equipment: it is half a Noah's Ark, full of living creatures, and also a modern laboratory with a thousand books and scientific instruments. For they have to take everything that a man needs for his body and mind with them into that empty, uninhabited world. The primitive equipment of primitive people, furs, skins and live animals, make strange partners here for the latest sophisticated modern devices. And the dual nature of the whole enterprise is as fantastic as the ship itself: an adventure, but one as calculated as a business deal, audacity with all the features of caution—endlessly precise and individual calculations against the even more endless whims of chance. They leave England on 1st June 1910. The British Isles are a beautiful sight at that time of year, with lush green meadows and the sun shining, warm and radiant in a cloudless sky. The men feel emotion as the coast vanishes behind them, for they all know that they are saying goodbye to warmth and sunlight for years, some of them perhaps for ever. But the British flag flies above the ship, and they console themselves by thinking that a signal from the world is travelling with them to the only part of the conquered earth that as yet has no master.

UNIVERSITAS ANTARCTICA

In January, after a short rest in New Zealand, they land at Cape Evans, on the rim of the eternal ice, and erect a building where they can spend the winter. In Antarctica December and January are the summer months, because only then does the sun shine in a white, metallic sky for a few hours of the day. The walls of their house are made of wood, like those of buildings erected by earlier expeditions, but inside the progress of time is evident. While their predecessors still made do with the dim and stinking light of smouldering fish-oil lamps, tired of their own faces, exhausted by the monotony of the sunless days, these twentieth-century men have the whole world and all its knowledge in abbreviated form inside their four walls. An acetylene lamp gives warm white light, as if by magic cinematography bringing them images of distant places, projections of tropical scenes from milder climates; they have a pianola for music, a gramophone provides the sounds of the human voice, their library contains the wisdom of their time. A typewriter clacks away in one room, another acts as a darkroom where cinematographic and coloured photographs are developed. The expedition's geologist tests stone for its radioactivity, the zoologist discovers new parasites on the penguins they catch, meteorological observations alternate with physical experiments. Every member of the expedition has his allotted work for the months of darkness, and a clever system transforms research in isolation into companionable study. For these thirty men give lectures every evening, hold university courses in the pack ice and the Arctic frost, and they acquire a three-dimensional view of the world in lively conversational exchange. The specialization of research gives up its pride here and promotes understanding in the company of others. In the middle of an elemental, primeval world, alone in a timeless place, thirty men instruct each other in the latest scientific findings of the twentieth century, and in their house they know not only the hour but the second of the world clock. It is touching to read how these serious men enjoy their Christmas tree and their spoof journal *The South Polar Times*, to find how some small incident—a whale surfacing, a pony's fall—becomes a major event, and on the other hand astonishing aspects of the expedition—the glow of the *aurora borealis*, the terrible frost, the vast loneliness—become ordinary daily experiences.

Now and then they venture on small outings. They try out their motor sledges, they learn to ski, they train the dogs. They equip a depot for the great journey, but the days on the calendar pass very slowly until summer (in December), when a ship reaches them through the pack ice with letters from home. Small groups also go on day-long journeys to toughen them up in the worst of the Antarctic winter, they try out their tents and consolidate their experiences. Not everything succeeds, but even the difficulties reinvigorate them. When they return from their expeditions, frozen and tired, they are welcomed back with rejoicing and a warm fire in the hearth, and the comfortable little house at latitude 77 seems to them, after days of deprivation, the most blessed place in the world.

But once such an expedition comes back from the west, and its news silences the house. On their way they have found Amundsen's winter quarters, and now Scott knows that, as well as the frost and danger, he has someone else competing with him for fame as the first to discover the secret of this refractory part of the earth: the Norwegian explorer Amundsen. He measures distances on the maps, and we can imagine his horror from what he wrote when he realized that Amundsen's winter quarters were 110 kilometres closer to the Pole than his own. He is shocked but does not despair. He writes proudly in his diary of his determination to press on for the honour of his country.

The name of Amundsen appears only once in the pages of Scott's diary, and never again. But the reader can feel that, from that day forward, a shadow of anxiety lies over the lonely house in the frozen landscape. And from now on there is not an hour when that name does not torment him, waking and sleeping.

SETTING OFF FOR THE POLE

A mile from the hut, on the hill where they take observations, they always post alternating guards. An apparatus resembling a cannon has been set up there—a cannon to combat an invisible enemy. Its purpose is to measure the first signs of warmth from the approaching sun. They wait for its appearance for days on end. Reflections already conjure up glowing colour in the morning sky, but the round disc of the sun does not yet rise to the horizon. However, that sky itself, full of the magical light of its proximity, the prelude to reflection, inspires the impatient men. At last the telephone on top of the hill rings, and they are happy to receive the news: the sun has risen, raising its head into the wintry night for an hour, for the first time in months. Its light is very faint, pale and wan, scarcely enough to enliven the icy air; the oscillating waves in the apparatus hardly produce any livelier signals, but the mere sight of the sun is cheering. The expedition is feverishly equipped to make use of the short span of light without delay, the light that means spring, summer and autumn in one, and in what, by our milder standards, would still be the depths of a bitter winter. The motor sledges race ahead. After them come the sledges drawn by Siberian ponies and dogs. The route has been carefully divided up into stages; a depot is set up at the end of every two days' journey to store new clothing and provisions for the return journey, and, most important of all, paraffin—condensed warmth in the endless frost. They move forward together, so as to return gradually in single groups, thus leaving behind the maximum load, the freshest draught animals and the best sledges for the final group, the chosen conquerors of the Pole.

The plan has been thought out in a masterly manner, even foreseeing accidents in detail. And there are indeed accidents.

After two days' journey the motor sledges break down and have to be left lying there, useless ballast. The ponies are not as tough as they might have expected either, but in this case organic triumphs over technical equipment: those that have to be shot provide the dogs with welcome, warm nourishment rich in blood to give them new energy.

They set out in separate groups on 1st November 1911. The photographs they took show the strange caravan consisting of first thirty, then twenty, then ten and finally only five men making their way through the white wilderness of a lifeless, primeval world. There is always a man going ahead, muffled up in furs and fabric, a being of wild, barbaric appearance with only his eyes and his beard showing. His hand, gloved in fur, holds a pony by the halter as it drags his heavily laden sledge along, and behind him comes another man in the same clothing and with the same attitude, followed by yet another, twenty black dots moving on in a line in that endless, dazzling white. At night they huddle in their tents, erecting ramparts of snow in the direction from which the wind is blowing to protect the ponies, and in the morning the march begins again, monotonous and dreary. They move through the icy air as it drinks human breath for the first time in millennia.

But there is more cause for concern. The weather remains poor: instead of going forty kilometres they can sometimes make only thirty, and every day is precious now they know that someone else is advancing towards the same destination from the other direction. Every small incident here becomes dangerous. A dog has run away, a pony will not eat—all these things are alarming, because values change so terrifyingly in this wilderness. The worth of every living creature here is multiplied by a thousand, is even irreplaceable. Immortality may depend on the four hooves of a single pony, a cloudy sky with a storm coming may prevent something for ever. And the men's own health is beginning to deteriorate: some have snow blindness, others have frostbitten limbs, the ponies are getting wearier all the time, and have to be kept short of food; and finally, just before the Beardmore Glacier, they collapse. The men have to do their sad duty: these brave animals, who have become their friends over two years here in isolation, and accordingly companionship, whom everyone knows by name and who have had affection lavished on them, must be killed. They call this sad place "Shambles Camp" because of the butchery that occurred there. Some members of the expedition split off at this bloodstained place and go back; the others brace themselves to make the last effort, the cruel way over the glacier, that dangerous wall of ice that surrounds the Pole, a wall that only the fire of a passionate human will can destroy.

The distance they march in a day is getting less and less, for the snow here forms a granulated crust, with the result that they have to haul the sledges rather than pull them along. The hard ice cuts the runners, the soft ice rubs the men's feet sore as they walk through its sandy consistency. But they do not give up. On 30th December they have reached 87 degrees latitude, Shackleton's ultimate point. Here the last group must turn back, leaving only five chosen members of the expedition to go on to the Pole. Scott looks at that last group. They dare not protest, but their hearts are heavy to think they must turn back so close to the destination and leave the glory of having seen the Pole first to their companions. But the dice have been cast. Once again they shake hands with each other, making a manly effort to hide their emotion, and then the final group turns. Two small, indeed tiny processions move on, one going south to the unknown, the other going north, homeward bound. Again and again, both groups look back to sense the last presence of living friends. Soon the last figure is out of sight. The five who have been chosen for the final stage of the journey go on into unknown territory: Scott, Bowers, Oates, Wilson and Evans.

THE SOUTH POLE

The accounts written by the five become uneasier in those last days; like the blue needle of the compass, they begin to tremble close to the Pole. "It is a big strain as the shadows creep slowly round from our right through ahead to our left!" But now and then hope sparkles more and more brightly. Scott describes the distances covered more and more feelingly. "Only another ninety miles to the Pole, but it's going to be a stiff pull both ways apparently." That is the voice of exhaustion. And two days later: "Only 63 miles from the Pole tonight. We ought to do the trick, but oh! for a better surface!" Then, however, we suddenly hear a new, victorious note. "Only 51 miles to the Pole tonight. If we don't get to it we shall be d—d close." On 14th January hope becomes certainty. "We are less than 40 miles from the Pole. It is a critical time, but we ought to pull through." On 14th January hope becomes cheerfulness in the account. You feel from Scott's heartfelt lines how tense their sinews are, tense with hope, how all their nerves quiver with expectation and impatience. The prize is close, they are already reaching out to the last mystery on earth. One final effort, and they will have reached their goal.

16TH JANUARY

"We started off in high spirits," Scott's diary entry begins. They set out in the morning, earlier than usual, roused from their sleeping bags by impatience to set eyes on the fearful and beautiful mystery as soon as they can. The five men, undeterred, cheerfully march twelve kilometres through the soulless, white wilderness; they cannot miss their destination now, they have almost done a great deed on behalf of mankind. But suddenly one of the companions, Bowers, becomes uneasy. His eye fixes on a small, dark point in the vast snowfield. He dares not put his suspicion into words, but by now the same terrible thought is shaking them all to the core: that signpost could be the work of human hands. They try ingenious means of reassuring themselves. Just as Robinson Crusoe tries in vain to take the strange footprint on the island for his own, they think they must be seeing a crevasse in the ice, or perhaps a reflection. With their nerves on edge they go closer, still trying to pretend to each other, although by now they all know the truth: the Norwegian Amundsen has reached the Pole before them.

Soon the last doubt is destroyed by the undeniable fact of a black flag hoisted on a sledge bearer above the traces of someone else's abandoned campsite—marks left by the runners of sledges, and dogs' paw prints. Amundsen has camped here. Something vast and hard for mankind to grasp has happened: in a molecule of time the South Pole of the earth, uninhabited for millennia, unseen by earthly eyes, has been discovered twice within two weeks. And they are the second discoverers—too late by a single month out of millions of months—the second men to reach the Pole, but coming first means everything to them and coming second nothing. So all their efforts were in vain, all their privations ridiculous, all the hopes of weeks, months, years were absurd. Scott wonders in his diary what it had all been for—for nothing but dreams? "All the day dreams must go; it will be a wearisome return." Tears come to their eyes, and in spite of their exhaustion they cannot sleep that night. Sad and hopeless, they set out like men condemned to death on the last march to the Pole that they had expected to conquer with jubilation. No one tries to console the others; they drag themselves on without a word. On 18th January Captain Scott reaches the Pole with his four companions. Now that the idea of having been the first no longer dazzles him, all he sees, dull-eyed, is the bleakness of the landscape. There is nothing there to be seen, Scott concludes, "very little that is different from the awful monotony of the past days. Great God! this is an awful place!" The only strange thing that they discover is created not by nature but by his rival's human hand: Amundsen's tent with the Norwegian flag fluttering boldly and triumphantly from the rampart that humanity has now stormed. A letter from the conqueror of the Pole waits for the unknown second comer who would tread here after him, asking him to forward it to King Haakon of Norway. Scott takes it upon himself to perform this hardest duty of all, acting as a witness to the world that someone else has done the deed that he longed to be his own.

They sadly put up the British flag, "our poor slighted Union Jack", beside Amundsen's sign of his victory. Then they leave "the goal of our ambition", Scott writes, with prophetic misgivings, "Now for the run home and a desperate struggle. I wonder if we can do it."

THE COLLAPSE

The dangers are ten times worse on the return journey. The compass guided them on the way to the Pole. Now they must also take care not to lose their own trail on the way back, not to lose it once for weeks on end, in case they miss finding the depots where they have stored their food, clothing and the warmth that a few gallons of petroleum mean. So they are uneasy about every step they take when driving snow impedes their vision, for every deviation from the trail will lead to certain death. And their bodies lack the freshness of the first march, when they were still heated by the chemical energies of plentiful food and the warmth of their Antarctic home.

Moreover, the steel spring of their will is slack now. On the outward journey the unearthly hope of representing the curiosity and longing of all mankind kept their energies heroically together, and they acquired superhuman strength through the consciousness of doing something immortal. Now they are fighting for nothing but to save their skins, their physical, mortal existence, for a less than glorious homecoming that perhaps they fear more than they desire.

The notes from those days make terrible reading. The weather gets worse and worse, winter has set in earlier than usual, and the soft snow forms a thick crust under their boots at an angle to the foot so that they stumble, and the frost wears down their weary bodies. There is always a little jubilation when they reach another depot after days of wandering and hesitation, and then a fleeting flame of confidence comes back into what they say. Nothing bears witness more finely to the intellectual heroism of these few men than the way that Wilson, the scientist, goes on making his observations even here, a hair's breadth from death, and adds sixteen kilograms of rare varieties of rock to all the necessary load on his own sledge.

But gradually human courage gives way to the superior power of nature, which here implacably, with the strength hardened by millennia, brings all the powers of cold, frost, snow and wind to bear against the five brave men. Their feet are badly injured now, and their bodies, inadequately warmed by one hot meal a day and weakened by scanty rations, are beginning to fail them. One day the companions are horrified to find that Evans, the strongest of them, is suddenly behaving strangely. He lags behind, keeps complaining of real and imaginary troubles; they are alarmed to conclude from his odd talk that the poor man has lost his mind as the result of a fall or of terrible pain. What are they to do with him? Leave him in this icy wilderness? But on the other hand they must reach the depot without delay, or else—Scott himself hesitates to write what would happen. The unfortunate Evans dies at 12.30 a.m. on 17th February, not a day's march from Shambles Camp where, for the first time, the slaughter of their ponies a month before provides them with a better meal.

The four men march on, but there is a disaster. The next depot brings more bitter disappointment. There is not enough oil there, and that means that they must be sparing with fuel, when warmth is the only real weapon against the cold. In the icy cold and stormy night, waking with a sense of discouragement, they hardly have the strength left to pull felt shoes on over their feet. But they drag themselves on, one of them, Oates, with frostbitten toes. The wind is blowing more sharply than ever, and at the next depot, on 2nd March, there is the cruel disappointment of again finding too little fuel to burn.

Now fear shows through the words they leave. We feel how Scott is attempting to hold back the horror, but again and again a shrill cry of despair disturbs the peace he tries to assume. "We cannot go on like this." Or, "One can only say, 'God help us!' and plod on our weary way." "Tragedy all along the line!" he writes, and wishes for Providence to come to their aid, since none can be expected from men.

However, they drag themselves on and on, without hope, gritting their teeth. Oates is getting worse and worse at keeping up with the others; he is more of a burden than a help to his friends. They have to delay their march at a midday temperature of minus forty-two degrees, and the unhappy man feels and knows that he is bringing death on his companions. They are already preparing for the end. Wilson, the scientist, hands out ten morphium tablets to each of them to hasten their end if necessary. They try one day's march more with their sick companion. Then the unfortunate man himself asks them to leave him behind in his sleeping bag and go on separately. They vigorously refuse, although they all realize that his suggestion would be a relief for them. Oates manages to go a little further on his frostbitten legs to their night quarters. He sleeps with them until next morning. When they wake and look out, there is a blizzard.

Suddenly Oates gets to his feet. "I am just going outside and may be some time," he tells his friends. The others tremble: they all know what that will mean. But no one dares say a word to stop him. No one dares to shake his hand one last time, for they all feel, with respect, that Captain Lawrence E.G. Oates of the Inniskilling Dragoons is going to his death like a hero.

Three weary, weakened men drag themselves through the endless, icy, iron-hard wilderness, tired and hopeless, with only the dull instinct of self-preservation stiffening their sinews to a stumbling walk. The weather gets worse and worse, a new disappointment mocks them at every depot, there is never enough oil, enough warmth. On 21st March they are only eighteen kilometres away from a depot, but the wind is blowing so murderously that they cannot leave their tent. Every evening they hope for the next morning, so as to reach their destination, for meanwhile their provisions are running out and with them their last hope. Their heating fuel is finished, and the thermometer says forty degrees below zero. Every hope is extinguished; they now have only the choice between starving or freezing to death. The three men struggle against the inevitable end for eight days in a small tent in the middle of the white wilderness world. On 29th March they know that no miracle can save them now. So they decide not to go another step towards their fate, but wait proudly for death as they have suffered every other misfortune. They crawl into their sleeping bags, and not a sigh reaches the outside world to speak of their last suffering.

THE DYING MAN'S LETTERS

In those moments, facing invisible but now imminent death while the blizzard attacks the thin walls of the tent like a madman, Captain Scott remembers all to whom he is close. Alone in the iciest silence, silence never broken by a human voice, he is heroically aware of his fraternal feelings for his country, for all mankind. In this white wilderness, a mirage of the mind conjures up the image of all who were ever linked to him by love, loyalty and friendship, and he addresses them. Captain Scott writes with freezing fingers, writes letters at the hour of his death to all the living men and women he loves.

They are wonderful letters. In the mighty presence of death all that is small and petty is dismissed; the crystalline air of that empty sky seems to breathe through his words. They are meant for individuals, but speak to all mankind. They are written at a certain time, they speak for eternity.

He writes to his wife, asking her to take good care of his son, the best legacy he can leave her, and above all, he says, "he must guard and you must guard him against indolence. Make him into a strenuous man." Of himself he says—at the end of one of the greatest achievements in the history of the world—"I had to force myself into being strenuous, as you know—had always an inclination to be idle." Even so close to death he does not regret but approves of his own decision to go on the expedition. "What lots and lots I could tell you of this journey. How much better it has been than lounging in too great comfort at home."

And he writes in loyal comradeship to the wife of one of his companions in misfortune, to the mother of another, men who will have died with him when the letters reach home, bearing witness to their heroism. Although he is dying himself, he comforts the bereaved families of the others with his strong, almost superhuman sense of the greatness of the moment and the memorable nature of their deaths.

And he writes to his friends, speaking modestly for himself but with a fine sense of pride for the whole nation, whose worthy son he feels himself to be at this moment. "I may not have proved a great explorer," he admits, "but I think [this diary] will show that the spirit of pluck and the power to endure has not passed out of our race." And death now impels him to tell one friend what manly reserve and his own modesty has kept him from saying all his life. "I never met a man in my life whom I loved and admired more than you, but I never could show you how much your friendship meant to me, for you had much to give and I had nothing."

He writes one last letter, the finest of all, to the British nation, feeling bound to give a reckoning of what he did for the fame of the country on the expedition, blaming only misfortune for its end. He enumerates the various accidents that conspired against him, and in a voice to which the echo of death lends pathos he calls on "our countrymen to see that those who depend upon us are properly cared for".

His last thought is not of his own fate, but of the lives of others. "For God's sake look after our people." The remaining pages are blank.

Captain Scott kept his diary until the last moment, when his fingers were so frozen that the pencil slipped out of them. Only the hope that the pages he had written would be found with his body, as a record of what he had done and of the courage of his countrymen, enabled him to make such a superhuman effort. The last thing he wrote, his frozen fingers shaking, was, "Send this diary to my wife." But then, in cruel certainty, he crossed out the words "my wife", and wrote over them the terrible "my widow".

THE ANSWER

For weeks their companions had waited in the hut. First confidently, then with some concern, finally with growing uneasiness. Expeditions were sent out twice to help them, but the weather beat them back.

The leaderless men spend all the long winter in the hut, at a loss, with the black shadow of the disaster falling on their hearts. Captain Robert Scott's achievement and his fate are locked in snow and silence during those months. The ice holds him and his last companions sealed in a glass coffin; not until 29th October, in the polar spring, does an expedition set out at least to find the heroes' bodies and the message they left. They reach the tent on 12th November, and find the bodies frozen in their sleeping bags, Scott with a fraternal arm round Wilson even in death. They also find the letters and documents, and dig the tragic heroes a grave. A plain black cross on top of a mound of snow now stands alone in the white world, hiding under it for ever the evidence of a heroic human achievement.

Or no! The expedition's achievements are wonderfully and unexpectedly resurrected, a miracle of our modern technological world. The dead men's friends bring back the records of the expedition on disks and films, the images are developed in a chemical bath, and Scott can be seen again walking with his companions in the polar landscape that only the other explorer, Amundsen, has seen. The news of his words and letters leaps along the electric wire into the astonished world; the king bows his knee in memory of the heroes in a British cathedral. And so what seemed to have been in vain bears fruit again, what appeared to be left undone is applauded as mankind's efforts to reach the unattainable. In a remarkable reversal, greater life comes from a heroic death; downfall arouses the will to rise to infinity. Chance success and easy achievement kindle only ambition, but the heart rises in response to a human being's fight against an invincibly superior power of fate, the greatest of all tragedies, and one that sometimes inspires poets and shapes life a thousand times over.

THE SEALED TRAIN

LENIN

---

9 April 1917

THE MAN WHO LODGES IN THE COBBLER'S HOUSE

In the years 1915, 1916, 1917 and 1918 the little island of peace that is Switzerland, surrounded on all sides by the stormy tide of the World War, is the ongoing scene of an exciting detective story. The envoys of enemy powers, who only a year before used to play friendly games of bridge together and visit one another's houses, now pass in the country's luxury hotels as if they had never met before. A whole flock of inscrutable characters steal in and out of their rooms: parliamentary deputies, secretaries, attachés, businessmen, veiled or unveiled ladies, all of them on secret missions. Magnificent limousines bearing foreign emblems of distinction draw up outside the hotels, to disgorge industrialists, journalists, virtuosos and people ostensibly travelling for pleasure. But almost all of them have the same task in mind: to find something out, to act as spies. And the porters who show them to their rooms, the chambermaids who sweep the rooms, have all been urged to keep their eyes open and be on the alert. Organizations are working against each other everywhere, in restaurants, boarding houses, post offices and cafés. What is described as propaganda is half espionage, what purports to be love is betrayal, and every openly conducted business deal done by these arrivals hastily passing through has a second or third deal hidden behind it. Everything is reported, everything is under surveillance; no sooner does a German of any rank set foot in Zürich than his enemy's embassy in Berne knows it, and so does Paris an hour later. Day after day, agencies large and small send whole volumes of reports both true and fictitious to the attachés, and the attachés send them on. All the walls are transparent as glass, telephones are tapped, correspondence is reconstructed from waste-paper baskets and sheets of blotting paper, and in the end there is such pandemonium that many of those involved no longer know whether they are hunters or hunted, spies or spied on, betrayed or betrayers.

But in those days there are few reports on one man, perhaps because he is too unimportant and does not stay at the grand hotels or go to the cafés, does not attend propaganda lectures, but lives with his wife in a cobbler's house and stays out of the limelight. His lodgings are on the second floor of one of the solidly built houses in the narrow old winding Spiegelgasse, across the River Limmat, a house with an arched roof, dark with smoke partly because of time, partly because there is a little sausage factory down in its yard. His neighbours are a baker's wife, an Italian and an Austrian actor. His landlady knows little about him except that he is not very talkative, just that he is a Russian with a name that is difficult to pronounce. She deduces, from the frugal meals and well-worn clothes of the couple, whose household belongings hardly fill the little basket they brought with them when they moved in, that he left his native land many years ago and does not have much money, or a very profitable occupation.

This small, stocky man is inconspicuous, and lives in as

inconspicuous a style as possible. He avoids company, and the other lodgers in the house seldom see the shrewd, dark look in the narrow slits of his eyes. He seldom has visitors. But at nine in the morning he regularly goes to the library and sits there until it closes at twelve. At ten past twelve exactly he is home again, and at ten past one he leaves the house so as to be the first reader back in the library, where he sits until six in the evening. However, as the news agencies pay attention only to those who talk a lot, they are not aware that solitary men who read and learn a great deal are always the most dangerous when it comes to instigating rebellion, so they write no news stories about the inconspicuous character who lodges at the cobbler's house. In socialist circles, he is known to have been the editor of a small radical journal for Russian émigrés, and in Petersburg as the leader of some kind of indescribable special party; but as he speaks harshly and contemptuously of the most highly regarded socialists, calling their methods erroneous, as it is difficult to get to know him, and he is not at all accommodating, no one bothers much about him. At most fifteen to twenty people, most of them young, attend the meetings that he sometimes holds in the evening in a small proletarian café, and so this loner is regarded as just one of those emigrant Russians whose feelings run high on a diet of much tea and long discussions. But no one thinks the small, stern-voiced man is of any significance, not three dozen people in Zürich consider it important to make a note of the name of Vladimir Ilyich Ulyanov who lodges in the cobbler's house. And if, at the time, one of those fine limousines racing at top speed from embassy to embassy had accidentally knocked him down in the street and killed him, the world would not know him by the name of either Ulyanov or Lenin.

FULFILMENT...

One day—it is the 15th of March 1917—the librarian of the Zürich library has a surprise. The hands of the clock say it is nine in the morning, and the place where the most punctual of all readers in the library sits every day is empty. The clock face shows nine-thirty, then ten; the tireless reader does not come in and will never visit the library again. For on the way there a Russian friend hailed him, or rather assailed him, with the news that the revolution has broken out in Russia.

At first Lenin can't believe it. It is as if he were numbed by the news. But then he hurries off, taking short, sharp strides, to the kiosk by the banks of the lake, and he waits there and outside the editorial offices of the newspaper hour after hour, day after day. It is true. The news is true, and with every passing day, so far as he is concerned, will become, magnificently, even truer. At first it is only the rumour of a palace revolution, apparently just a change of ministers; then comes the deposition of the Tsar; the appointment of a provisional government, the Duma; freedom for Russia and an amnesty for political prisoners—everything he has dreamt of for years, everything he has been working for over the last twenty years, in a secret organization, in his prison cell, in Siberia, in exile, it has all come true. All at once, it seems to him that the millions of dead demanded by this war did not die in vain. Their deaths no longer strike him as senseless, they were martyred in the cause of the new age of liberty and justice and eternal peace that is now dawning. Lenin, usually a man with such icy clarity of mind, a coldly calculating dreamer, is quite carried away by the news. And how the hundreds of others who sit in their little emigrant rooms in Geneva and Lausanne and Berne tremble, rejoicing at this happy turn of events: they can go home to Russia! Not travelling on forged passports, not entering the Tsar's realm under false names and in mortal danger, but as free citizens of a free country! They are already getting their scanty possessions ready, for the newspapers print Gorky's laconic telegram: they can all go home. They send letters and telegrams off in all directions to say they are on their way back. They must gather together, they must unite! Now they must stake their lives once again on the work to which they have dedicated themselves since their first waking hours: the Russian revolution!

...AND DISAPPOINTMENT

But after a few days they are full of consternation: the Russian revolution that made their hearts rise as if on eagles' wings is not the revolution they dreamt of, is not a Russian revolution at all. It was a palace revolt against the Tsar, instigated by British and French diplomats to prevent him from making peace with Germany, not a revolution of the people calling for peace and their rights. It is not the revolution they lived for and were ready to die for, but an intrigue of the parties favouring war, the imperialists and the generals who do not want to have their plans upset. And soon Lenin and those who think like him realize that the message promising them a safe return is not for all who want the real, the radical revolution of Karl Marx. Milyukov and the other liberals have given orders not to let them in. And while the moderates, the socialists who will be useful in prolonging the war, men like Plekhanov, are helpfully conveyed back to Petersburg by Britain in torpedo boats, with an official escort, Trotsky is kept in Halifax and the other radicals outside the Russian borders. At the borders of all the states of the *entente* there are blacklists of the names of all who attended the congress of the Third International in Zimmerwald. Lenin desperately sends telegram after telegram to Petersburg, but they are either intercepted or never delivered. What they do not know in Zürich, what almost no one knows in Europe, is very well known in Russia: how strong and energetic Vladimir Ilyich Lenin is, how purposeful and how murderously dangerous to his enemies.

The despair of those powerless radicals barred from Russia is unbounded. They have been planning their own Russian revolution for years and years, in countless General Staff meetings in London, Paris and Vienna. They have considered, assessed and discussed every detail of its organization. For decades in their journals they have weighed up against each other the theoretical and practical difficulties, dangers and opportunities. Lenin has spent his whole life considering this one complex of ideas, revising it again and again, bringing it to its final formulation. And now, because he is kept here in Switzerland, this revolution of his is to be watered down and wrecked by others, the idea of the liberation of the people, which is sacred to him, is to be put to the service of other nations and other interests. In a curious analogy, it is in those days that Lenin hears of the fate of Hindenburg in the first days of the war—Hindenburg, who has also manoeuvred and planned for his own Russian campaign, and when it breaks out has to stay at home in civilian clothing, following the progress of the generals called in and the mistakes they make on a map with little flags. Lenin, otherwise an iron-willed realist, entertains the most foolish and fantastic dreams in those days of despair. Could he not hire an aeroplane and fly to Russia over Germany or Austria? But the first man to offer his help turns out to be a spy. Lenin's ideas of flight become ever wilder and more chaotic. He writes to Sweden asking for a Swedish passport, saying he will pretend to be a mute so as not to be obliged to give information. Of course on the morning after these nights of fantasy Lenin himself always realizes that none of his crazy ideas can be carried out, but there is something else that he knows even in broad daylight—and that is that he must get back to Russia, he must put his own revolution into practice, the real and honourable revolution, not the political one. He must go back to Russia, and soon. Back at any price!

THROUGH GERMANY: YES OR NO?

Switzerland lies embedded between Italy, France, Germany and Austria. The route through the Allied countries is barred to Lenin as a revolutionary; the way through Germany and Austria is barred to him as a Russian subject, belonging to an enemy power. But, absurd as it may seem, Lenin can expect a friendlier reception from Kaiser Wilhelm's Germany than from Milyukov's Russia and the France of Poincaré. On the eve of America's declaration of war, Germany needs peace with Russia at any price. So a revolutionary making difficulties there for the envoys of Britain and France can only be a welcome aid.

However, it is a great responsibility to take such a step as suddenly entering into negotiations with imperial Germany, a country that he has threatened and abused over and over again in his writings. For in the light of all previous morality it is, naturally, high treason to enter and pass through an enemy country in the middle of war, and do so with the approval of the enemy's General Staff. Of course Lenin must know that it means he is initially compromising his own party and his own cause, that he will be suspect and sent back to Russia as the hired and paid agent of the German government, and that if he realizes his programme of bringing instant peace, he will always be blamed by history for standing in the way of the real, victorious peace of Russia. And of course not only the milder revolutionaries but also most of those who think as he does are horrified when he announces his readiness, if necessary, to take this dangerous and compromising course of action. They point out in dismay that negotiations were begun long ago by the Swiss Social Democrats to bring about the return of Russian revolutionaries by the legal and neutral method of an exchange of prisoners. But Lenin knows how tedious that course of action will be, how ingeniously and intentionally the Russian government will postpone their return *ad infinitum*, while he realizes that every day and every hour counts. He sees only the aim, while the others, being less cynical and less audacious, do not dare to decide on a course of action that by all existing laws and opinions is treacherous. But Lenin has made up his own mind, and takes on himself responsibility for negotiating with the German government.

THE PACT

It is for the very reason that Lenin knows how much attention this step will arouse, and how challenging it is, that he acts as openly as possible. On his behalf, the Swiss trades union secretary Fritz Platten goes to see the German ambassador, who had already negotiated in general with the Russian emigrants, and lays Lenin's conditions before him. For, as if that insignificant, unknown fugitive could already guess at his future authority, Lenin is not asking the German government for something, but stipulating the conditions on which the travellers would be ready to accept the co-operation of the German government. The railway carriage, he insists, must have an acknowledged right to extraterritoriality. There must be no checking of passports or persons at either the start or the end of the journey. The travellers will pay for their journey themselves, at the normal rates. No one would leave the carriage either if ordered to do so or acting on their own initiative. The minister, Romberg, passes these messages on. They reach the hands of Ludendorff, who undoubtedly approves them, although there is not a word in his memoirs about what was perhaps the most important decision of his life. The ambassador tries to make changes to many details, for Lenin has intentionally phrased the document so ambiguously that not only Russians but also an Austrian like Radek could travel in the train without any inspection. Like Lenin himself, however, the German government is in a hurry—for on that day, the 5th of April, the United States of America declares war on Germany.

And thus, on 6th April at midday, Fritz Platten receives the memorable decision: "This matter approved in the desired sense." On 9th April 1917, at two-thirty, a small, poorly dressed group carrying suitcases leave the Zähringerhof Restaurant on their way to Zürich Station. There are thirty-two of them in all, including women and children. Of the men, only the names of Lenin, Sinovyev and Radek are still known. They have eaten a modest lunch together, they have all signed a document saying that they are aware of the report in the French newspaper, *Le Petit Parisien*, that the Russian provisional government intends to treat the party travelling through Germany as guilty of high treason. They have signed in clumsy, awkward handwriting, saying that they take full responsibility for this journey upon themselves and have approved all the conditions. Quiet and determined, they now prepare for their historic journey.

Their arrival at the station attracts no attention. No reporters or photographers have turned up. Who in Switzerland knows this Herr Ulyanov, the man in the crumpled hat, shabby coat and ridiculously heavy mountain shoes (he takes them as far as Sweden), in the middle of a group of men and women laden with baskets, silently and inconspicuously looking for seats in the train? They appear the same as anyone else on a walking tour: people from the Balkan states, Ruthenia and Romania often stop here in Zürich for a couple of hours' rest, sitting on their wooden cases, before going on to France and the coast, and so overseas. The Swiss Socialist Party, which has also approved of the journey, has sent no representative; only a couple of Russians have come to give the travellers a little food and messages to take to the homeland, and a few also to try to dissuade Lenin, at the last minute, from going on this "pointless, treacherous journey". But the decision has been taken. At ten past three the guard of the train gives the signal. And the train rolls away to Gottmadingen, the German border station. Ten past three, and since then the world clock has shown a different time.

THE SEALED TRAIN

Millions of deadly shots were fired in the Great War, the weightiest, most powerful and far-reaching projectiles ever devised by ballistics engineers. But no shot went farther and was more fateful in modern history than the train that, carrying the most dangerous and determined revolutionaries of the century, races from the Swiss border across the whole of Germany to arrive in Petersburg, where it will blow the order of that time to pieces.

In Gottmadingen this unique projectile stands on the rails, a carriage of second- and third-class seats, with the women and children in second class and the men in third class. A chalk line on the floor marks off the area over which the Russians rule as a neutral zone, distinct from the compartment occupied by two German officers who are escorting this cargo of live explosive. The train rolls through the night without incident. Only in France do German soldiers, who have heard of Russian revolutionaries passing through, suddenly race up, and once an attempt made by German Social Democrats to communicate with the travellers is repelled. Lenin must know how he will expose himself to suspicion if he exchanges a single word with a German on German soil. They are welcomed ceremoniously in Sweden, and fall hungrily on the Swedish breakfast table, which serves a smorgasbord that seems to them like an improbable miracle. Then Lenin has to buy shoes to replace his heavy mountain boots, and a few clothes. At last they have reached the Russian border.

THE PROJECTILE TAKES OFF

The first thing Lenin does on Russian soil is typical of him: he does not see individual people, but makes for the newspapers. He has not been in Russia for fourteen years, he has not seen the earth of his country, its flag or the uniform of its soldiers. But this iron-hard ideologist does not burst into tears like the others, does not, like the women in the party, embrace the surprised and unsuspecting soldiers. First the newspaper,

Pravda, he wants to search it and see whether the paper, *his* paper, keeps to the international standpoint with sufficient determination. Angrily, he crumples it up. No, it does not; there is still too much about the motherland, too much patriotism, still not enough that, as he sees it, is purely revolutionary. It is time he came back, he thinks, to take the helm and impel the idea of his life towards victory or downfall. But will he get the chance? Won't Milyukov have him arrested as soon as he is in Petrograd—as the city is not yet called, but soon will be? The friends who have come to meet him are now in the train, Kamenev and Stalin, wearing strange, mysterious smiles in the dark third-class compartment, dimly lit by a light running low. They do not or will not answer his question.

But the answer given by reality is phenomenal. As the train runs into Finland Station the huge concourse is full of tens of thousands of workers, guards of honour carrying all kinds of weapons are waiting for the home-coming exile, the *Internationale* rings out. And as Vladimir Ilyich Ulyanov steps out of the train, the man who the day before yesterday was still living in the cobbler's house is seized by hundreds of hands and hoisted up on an armoured car. Floodlights are shone on him from the buildings and the fortress, and from the armoured car he makes his first speech to the people. The streets resound, and soon the "ten days that shake the world" have begun. The shot has hit its mark, destroying an empire, a world.

WILSON'S FAILURE

THE TREATY OF VERSAILLES

28 June 1919

O N 13TH DECEMBER 1918 the mighty steamer *George Washington*, with President Woodrow Wilson on board, is on its way to the European coast. Never since the beginning of the world has a single ship been awaited with so much hope and confidence by so many millions of people. The nations of Europe have been fighting each other furiously for four years; hundreds of thousands of their best young men, still in the bloom of youth, have been slaughtered on both sides with machine guns and cannon, flame-throwers and poison gas; for four years they have expressed nothing in speech or on paper but hatred and vituperation for each other. But all the bad feeling whipped up could not silence an inner voice that told them that what they said, what they did, dishonoured our present century. All these many people, consciously or unconsciously, had a secret feeling that mankind had retreated headlong into chaotic centuries of a barbarism thought to be dead and gone long ago.

Then, from the other side of the world in America, a voice spoke out clearly above battlefields still hot with blood, demanding "never war again". Never discord again, never the criminal old style of secret diplomacy that had driven nations to the slaughter without their knowledge or volition, but instead a new, better world order, "the reign of law, based upon the consent of the governed and sustained by the organized opinion of mankind". And remarkably, that voice was understood at once in all countries and all languages. The war, yesterday still a pointless quarrel about tracts of land, borders, raw materials, ore mines and oilfields, had suddenly taken on a higher, almost religious meaning: eternal peace, the messianic empire of law and humanity. All of a sudden it no longer seemed as if the blood of millions had been shed in vain: this one generation had suffered only so that such suffering would never be seen on earth again. Hundreds of thousands, millions of voices, in the grip of frenzied confidence, summoned this man; Wilson was to make peace between the victors and the defeated, and ensure that it would be a just peace. Like another Moses he, Wilson, was to bring the tablets of the new League of Nations to the peoples who had gone astray. Within a few weeks the name of Woodrow Wilson becomes a religious, a messianic power. Streets, buildings and children are named after him. Every nation that feels in need or at a disadvantage sends delegates to him. The letters and telegrams with suggestions, requests and adjurations from all quarters of the globe arrive in their thousands and thousands, building up until whole crates of them are carried aboard the ship going to Europe. A whole part of the earth, the whole world unanimously demands this man as the arbitrator of its last quarrel before the final reconciliation of which it dreams.

And Wilson cannot defy the summons. His friends in America advise him against going to the peace conference in person. As President of the United States, they say, it is his duty not to leave his country; he would do better to conduct negotiations from a distance. But Woodrow Wilson is not to be dissuaded. Even the highest position in his country, the presidency of the United States, seems to him a small thing beside the task incumbent on him. He wants to serve not a country, not a continent, but all mankind, and not this one moment but a better future. He doesn't want to be narrow-minded and act only in the interests of America, for "interest does not bind men together, interest separates men". Rather, he wants to serve the advantage of all. He himself, he feels, must take care that military men and diplomats do not appropriate national passions again: the union of mankind would mean the death knell for their fatal professions. He must be the guarantee, in person, that "the will of the people rather than that of their leaders" is heard, and every word is to be spoken before the whole world, with doors and windows open at that congress of peace, the last, the final peace congress of mankind.

So he stands on the ship and looks at the European coast emerging from the mist, vague and formless like his own dream of the future brotherhood of nations. He stands erect, a tall man with firm features, his eyes keen and clear behind his glasses, his chin thrust forward with typically American energy, but his full, fleshy lips are closed. The son and grandson of Presbyterian pastors, he has the strength and restricted vision of those men for whom there is only one truth, and who are sure that they know what it is. He has the fervour of all his pious Scottish and Irish ancestors in his blood, and the enthusiasm of the Calvinist faith that sets a leader and teacher the task of saving sinful humanity, not to mention the obstinacy of those heretics and martyrs who would rather be burnt for their convictions than deviate one iota from the word of the Bible. And to him, as a Democrat and a scholar, the concepts of humanity, mankind, liberty, freedom and human rights are not cold words but what the gospel was to his forefathers. To him, they mean not vague, ideological concepts, but articles of religious faith, and he is determined to defend every syllable of them as his ancestors defended the message of the evangelists. He has fought many battles, but this one, he feels as he looks at the land of Europe becoming ever clearer before his eyes, will be the deciding one. Instinctively, he tenses his muscles "to fight for the new order, agreeably if we can, disagreeably if we must".

But soon the severity leaves his gaze as he looks into the distance. The cannon and flags that greet him in Brest harbour are merely honouring the president of an allied republic, but the noise he hears from the shore is, he feels, not an artificial, organized reception, not a pretence of jubilation, but the blazing enthusiasm of a whole nation. Wherever the train in which he is travelling goes, flags wave—the flames of hope—from every village, every hamlet, every house. Hands reach out to him, voices roar around him, and as he is driven into Paris down the Champs-Élysées, cascades of enthusiasm fall from the living walls. The people of Paris, the people of France, as the symbol of all the distant nations of Europe, are shouting jubilantly, they press their expectations on him. His face relaxes more and more, his teeth flash in a free, happy, almost intoxicated smile, and he waves his hat to right and left as if to greet them all and the whole world. Yes, he did right to come himself; only the vigorous will can triumph over the rigidity of the law. Can one, should one not create such a happy city and such joyfully hopeful men and women for everyone, to last for ever? One night for rest and quiet, and then he will begin the work of giving the world the peace it has dreamt of for thousands of years, thus doing the greatest deed that a human being has ever accomplished.

Journalists flock impatiently to the exterior of the palace that the French government has set aside for his use, to the corridors of the Foreign Ministry, to the Hôtel de Crillon, headquarters of the American delegation. They are an army of some size in themselves. A hundred and fifty have come from North America alone; every country, every city has sent its correspondents, and they are clamouring for tickets to let them into all the meetings. All of them! For "complete publicity" has been promised to the world. There are to be no secret meetings or agreements this time. The first of the fourteen points runs, word for word, that there shall be "open covenants of peace, openly arrived at, after which there shall be no private international understandings of any kind". The pestilence of secret agreements, which has demanded more deaths than all other epidemics, is to be defeated once and for all by the new salve of Wilson's "open diplomacy".

But, to their disappointment, the impetuosity of the journalists comes up against delaying tactics. Yes, certainly, they would all be given access to the large meetings, and the minutes of those public meetings—in reality, chemically cleaned of all causes of tension—would be conveyed to the world in full. But no information could be given yet. First the method of procedure had to be established. Disappointed, those who wanted to know more felt that there was some inconsistency here. However, they had not actually been told anything untrue. It was over the method of procedure that Wilson sensed the resistance of the Allies at the first discussion between the Big Four; they did not all want to negotiate openly, and with good reason. Secret agreements lie in the files and records of all military nations, agreements ensuring that they all get their share of the booty. There is dirty laundry that can be mentioned only in a very restricted circle. If the whole conference were not to be compromised from the first, these matters had to be discussed behind closed doors and sanitized. However, there were differences of opinion not only in the method of procedure but also at a deeper level. Fundamentally, the situation was entirely unambiguous in both groups, the American and the European, a clear opinion on the right, a clear opinion on the left. It was not just that peace was to be made at this conference; there were really two peaces to be made, two entirely different treaties. One peace was to end the war with defeated Germany, which had laid down its arms, and at the same time another, the peace of the future, was to make any future war impossible for ever. On one hand peace of the old, hard kind, on the other the new Wilsonian covenant that was to found the League of Nations. Which was to be negotiated first?

Here both points of view come up sharply against each other. Wilson takes little interest in peace only for the present day. Determining borders, paying compensation, making war reparations and so forth should, as he saw it, be left to the experts and committees on the basis of the principles established in the fourteen points. That was painstaking, detailed work, subsidiary work, work for experts on the subjects. The task of the leading statesmen of the time, on the other hand, should, and he hoped would, be what was new and coming into being, the union of nations, eternal peace. To each group, its own ideas are of pressing importance. The European Allies reasonably make the point that the exhausted and battered world cannot be left waiting months for peace to be made, or Europe will succumb to chaos. First they must get tangible matters settled, the borders, the reparations. Men still carrying arms must be sent back to their wives and children, currencies must be stabilized, trade and commerce must get going again, and only then, on an established basis, can the mirage of Wilson's project be allowed to shine brightly. Just as Wilson is not really interested in peace for its own sake, Clemenceau, Lloyd George, Sonnino, as practical men and tacticians, are really indifferent to Wilson's demands. They have paid tribute to his humane requirements and his ideas out of political calculation, and in part also out of genuine sympathy, because, whether consciously or unconsciously, they feel the captivating, compelling force of an unselfish principle on their nations; they are therefore willing to discuss his plan, qualified and watered-down to some extent. But first, however, peace with Germany as the conclusion of the war, then the covenant.

However, Wilson himself is practical enough to know how delay can affect a vital demand, leeching away its force. He himself knows how you can postpone matters by means of annoying interruptions; no one gets to be President of the United States by idealism alone. So he inflexibly insists on his own viewpoint: the covenant must be worked out first, and he even demands its explicit verbal inclusion in the peace treaty with Germany. A second conflict crystallizes organically from this demand. As the Allies see it, building such principles into the treaty would mean granting Germany the undeserved reward of the principles of humanity in advance, after it was the guilty party that brutally infringed international law by invading Belgium, and set a terrible example of ruthlessness in General Hoffmann's negotiations at Brest-Litovsk, when Russia backed out of the Great War after the revolution. They insist on settling accounts first in the old way, in hard cash, and only then turning to the new method. Fields still lie devastated, whole cities are destroyed by gunfire. To make an impression on Wilson, the Europeans urge him to go to see them for himself. But Wilson, that "impractical man", deliberately looks past the ruins. His eyes are fixed on the future, and he sees not the cities wrecked by cannon but the everlasting construction to come. He has one task and one only: to "do away with an old order and establish a new one". Imperturbable and implacable, he persists with his demand, in spite of the protests of his own advisers Lansing and House. First the covenant. First the cause of all mankind, only then the interests of the individual nations.

It is a hard battle and it wastes a great deal of time—something that will prove disastrous. Woodrow Wilson has unfortunately omitted to define his dreams more clearly in advance. The project of the covenant that he puts forward is by no means entirely formulated, it is only a first draft, and it has to be discussed, altered, improved, reinforced or watered down at countless meetings. In addition, courtesy requires him to make visits now and then to Paris and the other capital cities of his allies. So Wilson goes to London, speaks in Manchester, visits Rome; and as the other statesmen show no enthusiasm for making progress with his project in his absence, more than a whole month has been lost before the first plenary session is held—a month during which regular and irregular troops improvise battles in Hungary and Romania, Poland and the Baltic area, occupying land, while there is a rising rate of famine in Vienna and the situation in Russia is considerably worse.

But even in this first plenary session on 18th January, it is only determined in theory that the covenant is to form "an integral part of the general treaty of peace". The document itself has not yet been drafted, it is still going from hand to hand in endless discussions. Another month goes by, a month of the most terrible unrest for Europe, which more and more clearly wants to have its real, actual peace. Not until 14th February 1919, a quarter of a year after the Armistice, can Wilson put forward the covenant in its final form, the form in which it is unanimously accepted.

Once again the world rejoices. Wilson has won his cause. In future, peace will not be kept by terror and the force of arms, but by agreement and belief in a higher law. Wilson is stormily acclaimed as he leaves the palace. Once again, for the last time, he looks with a proud, grateful smile of delight at the crowd surrounding him, sensing other nations behind this one. And behind this generation that has suffered so much he sees future generations who, thanks to this ultimate safeguard, will never again feel the scourge of war and the humiliation of dictators and dictatorships. It is the greatest day of his life, and at the same time his last happy day. For Wilson spoils his own victory by leaving the battlefield too early; and next day, 15th February, he travels back to America, to place the Magna Carta of eternal peace before his voters and countrymen, before returning to sign the other peace treaty, the last, the treaty to put an end to war.

Yet again the cannon thunder in salute as the *George Washington* moves away from Brest, but already the throng watching the ship leave is less dense and more indifferent. Something of the great, passionate tension, something of the messianic hope of the nations has already worn off as Wilson leaves Europe. He also meets with a cool reception in New York. No airplanes circle the ship coming home, there is no stormy, loud rejoicing, and in his own offices, in the Senate, in Congress, within his own party, the welcome is rather wary. Europe is dissatisfied, feeling that Wilson has not gone far enough. America is dissatisfied, feeling that he has gone too far. To Europe, his commitment to the reconciliation of conflicting interests in the general interest of mankind does not yet seem far-reaching enough; in America his political opponents, who already have their eyes on the next presidential election, are agitating because, they say, he has linked the new continent too closely, without justification, to the restless and unpredictable continent of Europe, thus contravening a fundamental principle of national policy, the Monroe Doctrine. Woodrow Wilson is forcefully reminded that it is not for him to found the future empire of his dreams, or think for other nations, but to keep in mind first and foremost the Americans, who elected him to represent what they themselves want. Still exhausted from the European negotiations, Wilson has to enter into new negotiations with both his own party representatives and his political opponents. Above all, he must retrospectively build a back door into the proud structure of the covenant that he thought he had constructed to be inviolable and impregnable, the dangerous "provision for the withdrawal of America from the League", allowing the United States to back out at any time they liked. That means the removal of the first stone from the structure of the League of Nations, planned to last for all eternity; the first crack in the wall has opened. It is a fatal flaw that will ultimately be responsible for its collapse.

Wilson does succeed in carrying through his new Magna Carta in America as he did in Europe, if with reservations and corrections, but it is only half a victory. He travels back to Europe, not in as free and confident a mood as he first left his country, to perform the second part of his task. Once again the ship makes for Brest, but he no longer bends the same hopeful gaze as before on the shore of France. In these few weeks he has become older and wearier because he is more disappointed, his features are sterner and tauter, a harsh and grim line begins to show around his mouth, now and then a tic runs over his left cheek, an ominous sign of the sickness gathering within him. The doctor who is travelling with him takes every opportunity to warn him to spare himself. A new and perhaps even harder battle lies ahead. He knows that it is more difficult to carry through principles than to formulate them. But he is determined not to sacrifice any part of his programme. All or nothing. Eternal peace or none at all.

There is no jubilation now when he lands, no rejoicing in the streets of Paris. The newspapers are cool as they wait to see what happens, the people are cautious and suspicious. The truth of Goethe's dictum to the effect that "Enthusiasm, unlike a pickle / Does not keep well, but may prove fickle" is felt once again. Instead of exploiting the hour while things were going well, instead of striking while the iron was hot, yielding and malleable, Wilson allowed Europe's idealistic disposition to cool off. That one month of his absence has changed everything. Lloyd George left the conference at the same time as he did. Clemenceau, injured by a pistol shot fired by a would-be assassin, has been unable to work for two months, and the backers of private interests have used those unsupervised moments to force their way into the meeting rooms of the committees. The military men have worked most energetically and are the most dangerous. All the field marshals and generals who have been in the limelight for years—whose words, whose decisions, whose arbitrary will made hundreds of thousands do as they wanted for four years—are not in the least inclined to retire into obscurity. Their very existence is threatened by a covenant depriving them of their means of power, the armies, by stating that its purpose is "to abolish conscription and all other forms of compulsory military service". So all this drivel about eternal peace, which would rob them of the point of their profession, must, at all costs, be eradicated or sidelined. They menacingly demand armament instead of Wilson's disarmament, new borders and international guarantees instead of the supra-national solution. You cannot, they say, ensure the welfare of a country with fourteen points plucked out of the air, only by providing your own army with weapons and disarming your enemies. Behind the militarists come the representatives of industrialists who keep the machinery of war running, the go-betweens who plan to do well out of reparations; while the diplomats, being threatened behind their backs by the opposition parties, and all of them wanting to acquire a good tract of land for their own countries, are increasingly hesitant. A clever touch or so on the keyboard of public opinion, and all the European newspapers, backed by their American counterparts, are playing variations in their various languages on the same theme: Wilson's fantasies are delaying peace. His Utopian ideas, they proclaim, while very praise-worthy in themselves and full of the spirit of idealism, have been standing in the way of the consolidation of Europe. No more time must be lost over moral scruples and supra-moral consideration for others! If peace is not made immediately then chaos will break out in Europe.

Unfortunately, these accusations are not entirely unjusti-fied. Wilson, who is thinking of the centuries ahead, does not measure time by the same standards as the nations of Europe.

Four or five months do not seem to him much to spend on a task that aims to realize a dream thousands of years old. But meanwhile the private armies known as *Freikorps*, organized by dark powers, are marching in the east of Europe; occupied territories, large tracts of land do not yet know where they belong and which country they are to be a part of. After four months, the German and Austrian delegations still have not been received; nations are restless behind borders as yet undrawn; there are clear and ominous signs that in desperation Hungary will be handed over to the Bolshevists tomorrow and Germany the day after tomorrow. So there must be a result soon, there must be a treaty, clamour the diplomats, whether it is a just or an unjust one, and every obstacle to that treaty must be cleared away, first and foremost the unfortunate covenant!

Wilson's first hour in Paris is enough to show him that everything he built up in three months has been undermined in the single month of his absence, and now threatens to collapse. Marshal Foch has almost succeeded in getting the covenant eliminated from the peace treaty, and the work of the first three months seems to have been wasted for no good reason. But Wilson is firmly determined not to give any ground at all where the crucial points are concerned. Next day, on 15th March, he announces officially through the press that the resolution of 25th January is as valid as ever, and "that the covenant is to be an integral part of the treaty of peace". This declaration is his first measure to counter the attempt to have the treaty with Germany concluded not on the basis of the new covenant, but on the grounds of the old secret treaties between the Allied powers. President Wilson now knows exactly what those powers, who have only just solemnly sworn to respect self-determination by the nations, propose to demand. France wants the Rhineland and the Saar; Italy wants Fiume and Dalmatia; Romania, Poland and Czechoslovakia want their own share of the booty. If he does not resist, peace will be made by the old methods of Napoleon, Talleyrand and Metternich, methods that he has denounced, and not according to the principles he has laid down and that have been solemnly accepted.

Two weeks pass in bitter dispute. Wilson himself does not want to cede the Saar to France, because he regards this first breakthrough of self-determination as setting the example for all other assumptions. And in fact Italy, feeling that all its demands are bound up with the first to be conceded, is already threatening to walk out of the conference. The French press beats its drums all the harder, Bolshevism is pushing forward from Hungary and will soon, say the Allies, overrun the world. There is ever more tangible resistance to be felt even from Wilson's closest advisers, Colonel House and Robert Lansing. Once his friends, they are now advising him to make peace quickly in view of the chaotic state of the world; rather than chaos, they say, it would be better to sacrifice a few idealistic demands. A unanimous front has closed before Wilson, and public opinion is hammering away in America behind his back, stirred up by his political enemies and rivals. There are many times when Wilson feels he has exhausted his powers. He admits to a friend that he cannot hold out much longer on his own against everyone else, and says he is determined that if he cannot get what he wants he will leave the conference.

In the midst of this battle against everyone he is finally attacked by one last enemy, the enemy within, his own body. On 3rd April, just as the conflict of brutal reality against still-unformed ideals has reached a crucial point, Wilson's legs give way under him. An attack of influenza forces him, at the age of sixty-three, to take to his bed. However, the demands of time are even more pressing than those of his fevered blood, leaving the sick man no rest. Messages of disaster flash from a gloomy sky: on 5th April Communism comes to power in Bavaria. The Munich Socialist Republic is proclaimed in that city. At any time Austria, half starving and wedged between a Bolshevik Bavaria and a Bolshevik Hungary, could join them; with every hour of resistance this one man's responsibility for everyone grows. The exhausted Wilson is pestered even at his bedside. In the next room Clemenceau, Lloyd George and Colonel House are discussing the situation. They are all determined that they must come to some conclusion at any price. And Wilson is to pay that price in the form of his demands and his ideals; his notions of "enduring peace" must, all the other statesmen unanimously say, be deferred because they block the way to a real, material, military peace.

But Wilson—tired and exhausted, undermined by sickness and the attacks of the press, blamed for delaying peace, irritated and abandoned by his own advisers, pestered by the representatives of other governments—still will not give way. He feels that he must not go against his own word, and that he will be truly fighting for peace only if he can reconcile it with the non-military and enduring peace of the future, if he tries his utmost for the "world federation" that alone will save Europe. Scarcely on his feet again, he strikes a deciding blow. On 7th April he sends a telegram to the Navy Department in Washington: "What is the earliest possible date USS *George Washington* can sail for Brest France, and what is probable earliest date of arrival Brest. President desires movements this vessel expedited." On the same day the world learns that President Wilson has ordered the ship to come to Europe.

The news is like a clap of thunder, and is immediately understood. All round the world it is known that President Wilson refuses to accept any peace that runs counter to the principles of the covenant, even if only in one point, and is determined to leave the conference rather than give way. A historic moment has come, a moment that will determine the fate of Europe, the fate of the world for decades, indeed centuries. If Wilson rises from the conference table the old world order will collapse, and chaos will ensue; but perhaps it will be one of those states of chaos from which a new star is born. Europe shivers impatiently. Will the other participants in the conference take that responsibility? Will he take it himself? It is a moment of decision.

A moment of decision. In that moment Woodrow Wilson's mind is still firmly made up. No compromise, no yielding, no "hard peace", only the "just peace". The French will not get the Saar, the Italians will not get Fiume, there will be no carving-up of Turkey, no "bartering of peoples". Right must triumph over Might, the ideal over reality, the future over the present! *Fiat iustitia, pereat mundus.* Let there be justice, though the world should perish. That brief hour will be Wilson's greatest, most humane and heroic moment; if he has the power to endure it his name will be immortalized among the small number of true friends of humanity, and he will have an unparalleled achievement to his credit. But after that hour, after that moment there will be a week in which he is assailed from all sides. The French, British and Italian press accuse him, the peace-maker, the *eirenopoieis,* of destroying the peace by theoretically theological rigidity, and sacrificing the real world to a private Utopia. Even Germany, having hoped for so much from him, and now distraught at the outbreak of Bolshevism in Bavaria, turns against him. And no less than his own countrymen Colonel House and Lansing implore him to change his mind, while his private secretary Tumulty, who had wired encouragingly from Washington a few days earlier—"Only a bold stroke by the President will save Europe and perhaps the world"—now cables from the same city, when Wilson has made that bold stroke: "...Withdrawal most unwise and fraught with dangerous possibilities here and abroad... President should... place the responsibility for a break of the Conference where it properly belongs... A withdrawal at this time would be a desertion."

Dismayed, desperate, and with his confidence disturbed by this unanimous onslaught, Wilson looks around him. There is no one at his side, they are all against him in the conference hall, all his own staff too; and the voices of the invisible millions upon millions adjuring him from a distance to stand firm and be true to himself do not reach him. He does not guess that if he carried out his threat and stood up to leave he would make his name immortal for all time, that if he did remain true to himself he would bequeath that immaculate name to the future as a postulate constantly to be invoked. He does not guess what creative force would proceed from that "No" if he announced it to the powers of greed, hatred and stupidity, he feels only that he is alone and is too weak to shoulder that ultimate responsibility. And so, fatally, Wilson gradually gives way, he relaxes his rigid stance. Colonel House acts as go-between; concessions will be made, for a week the bargaining over borders goes this way and that. At last, on 15th April—a dark day in history—Wilson agrees with a heavy heart and a troubled conscience to the military demands of Clemenceau, which have already been considerably toned down: the Saar will not be handed over for ever, only for fifteen years. This is the uncompromising Wilson's first compromise, and as if by magic the mood of the Parisian press changes overnight. The newspapers that were yesterday condemning him as the disturber of the peace, the destroyer of the world, now praise him as the wisest of all statesmen. But that praise burns like a reproach in his inmost heart. Wilson knows that he may indeed have saved peace, the peace of the present day; but enduring peace in a spirit of reconciliation, the only kind that saves us, has been lost, the opportunity wasted. Lack of sense has conquered true sense, passion has conquered reason. The world, storming a supra-temporal ideal, has been beaten back, and he, the leader and standard-bearer of that ideal, has lost the deciding battle, the battle against himself.

Did Wilson do right or wrong in that fateful hour? Who can say? At least, a decision was made, and the historic day cannot be called back. Its effects reach far ahead over decades and centuries, and we are paying the price for the decision with our blood, our despair, our powerlessness against destruction. From that day on Wilson's power, in his own time an unparalleled moral force, was broken, his prestige gone and with it his strength. A man who makes a concession can no longer stop. Compromises inevitably lead to more compromises.

Dishonesty creates dishonesty, violence engenders more violence. The peace of which Wilson dreamt as a whole entity lasting for ever remains incomplete, because it was not formed with a mind to the future or out of the spirit of humanity and the pure material of reason. A unique opportunity, perhaps the most far-reaching in history, was pitifully wasted, and the disappointed world, deprived of any element of the divine again, in a sombre and confused mood, feels the lack of it. The man who goes home, and who was once hailed as the saviour of the world, is not anyone's saviour now, only a tired, sick person who has been mortally wounded. No jubilation accompanies him, no flags are waved. As the ship sets out from the European coast, the conquered man turns away. He will not let his eyes look back at our unfortunate continent, which has been longing for peace and unity for thousands of years and has never achieved it. And once again the eternal vision of a humane world recedes into mist and into the distance.

Pushkin Press

Pushkin Press was founded in 1997. Having first rediscovered European classics of the twentieth century, Pushkin now publishes novels, essays, memoirs, children's books, and everything from timeless classics to the urgent and contemporary.

Pushkin books like this one represent exciting, high-quality writing from around the world. Pushkin publishes widely acclaimed, brilliant authors such as Stefan Zweig, Marcel Aymé, Antal Szerb, Paul Morand and Yasushi Inoue, as well as some of the most exciting contemporary and often prize-winning writers, including Andrés Neuman, Edith Pearlman and Ryu Murakami.

Pushkin Press publishes the world's best stories, to be read and read again.

*

Héctor Abad	*Recipes for Sad Women*
Olivier Adam	*Cliffs*
Flavia Arzeni	*An Education in Happiness:*
	The Lessons of Hesse and Tagore
François Augiéras	*A Journey to Mount Athos*
	Journey of the Dead
	The Sorcerer's Apprentice
Marcel Aymé	*Beautiful Image*
	The Man Who Walked through Walls
Salim Bachi	*The New Adventures of Sinbad the Sailor*
	The Silence of Mohammed
Philippe Beaussant	*Rendezvous in Venice*
Andrei Bely	*Petersburg*
Olivier Berggruen	*The Writing of Art*
Eduardo Berti	*Agua*
Filippo Bologna	*How I Lost the War*
	The Parrots

MARELLA CARACCIOLO CHIA	*The Light in Between*
VELIBOR ČOLIĆ	*The Uncannily Strange and Brief Life of Amedeo Modigliani*
LOUIS COUPERUS	*Ecstasy*
	Eline Vere
	Inevitable
	Psyche
	The Hidden Force
RÉGIS DEBRAY	*Against Venice*
PENELOPE S. DELTA	*A Tale Without a Name*
CHARLES DICKENS	*Memoirs of Joseph Grimaldi*
ISAK DINESEN	*The Necklace and The Pearls*
ALAIN ELKANN	*Envy*
	The French Father
NICOLAS FARGUES	*I Was behind You*
MEDARDO FRAILE	*Things Look Different in the Light*
CARLOS GAMERRO	*An Open Secret*
GAITO GAZDANOV	*The Spectre of Alexander Wolf*
JULIEN GRACQ	*A Dark Stranger*
	Chateau d'Argol
JULIAN GREEN	*The Other Sleep*
BROTHERS GRIMM	*The Juniper Tree and Other Tales*
PIETRO GROSSI	*Fists*
	The Break
	Enchantment
EDUARDO HALFON	*The Polish Boxer*
PETER HANDKE	*A Sorrow Beyond Dreams*
HERMANN HESSE	*Hymn to Old Age*
E.T.A. HOFFMANN	*The Nutcracker and The Strange Child*
HUGO VON HOFMANNSTHAL	*Andreas*
YASUSHI INOUE	*Bullfight*
PASI ILMARI JÄÄSKELÄINEN	*The Rabbit Back Literature Society*
HENRY JAMES	*Letters from the Palazzo Barbaro*
	Letters to Isabella Stewart Gardner
PETER STEPHAN JUNGK	*The Inheritance*
ERLING KAGGE	*Philosophy for Polar Explorers*
SØREN KIERKEGAARD	*Diary of a Seducer*
PETR KRÁL	*In Search of the Essence of Place*
	Loving Venice
	Working Knowledge
MAXIM LEO	*Red Love: The Story of an East German Family*

ALEXANDER LERNET-HOLENIA	*I Was Jack Mortimer*
SIMON LIBERATI	*Anthology of Apparitions*
OLIVER MATUSCHEK	*Three Lives: A Biography of Stefan Zweig*
GUY DE MAUPASSANT	*The Necklace and The Pearls*
JEAN-EUPHÈLE MILCÉ	*Alphabet of the Night*
PAUL MORAND	*Hecate and Her Dogs*
	Tender Shoots
	The Allure of Chanel
	Venices
RYU MURAKAMI	*Popular Hits of the Showa Era*
	From the Fatherland, with Love
	Coin Locker Babies
	69
ANDRÉS NEUMAN	*Traveller of the Century*
AUÐUR AVA ÓLAFSDÓTTIR	*Butterflies in November*
UMBERTO PASTI	*The Age of Flowers*
EDITH PEARLMAN	*Binocular Vision*
EDGAR ALLAN POE	*The Journal of Julius Rodman*
ALEXANDER PUSHKIN	*The Queen of Spades*
RAYMOND RADIGUET	*Count d'Orgel*
	The Devil in the Flesh
ANTOINE DE SAINT-EXUPÉRY	*Letter to a Hostage*
GEORGE SAND	*Laura: A Journey into the Crystal*
FRIEDRICH VON SCHILLER	*The Man Who Sees Ghosts*
ARTHUR SCHNITZLER	*Casanova's Return to Venice*
	Dying
	Fräulein Else
ADOLF SCHRÖDER	*The Game of Cards*
LAURENT SEKSIK	*The Last Days*
WILLIAM SHAKESPEARE	*Sonnets*
NIHAD SIREES	*The Silence and the Roar*
JAN JACOB SLAUERHOFF	*The Forbidden Kingdom*
SIMONA SPARACO	*About Time*
ADALBERT STIFTER	*The Bachelors*
	Rock Crystal
ITALO SVEVO	*A Life*
ANTAL SZERB	*Journey by Moonlight*
	Love in a Bottle
	Oliver VII
	The Pendragon Legend
	The Queen's Necklace

FRIEDRICH TORBERG	*Young Gerber*
MARK TWAIN	*The Jumping Frog and Other Sketches*
ELLEN ULLMAN	*By Blood*
	Close to the Machine
	The Bug
LOUISE DE VILMORIN	*Madame de*
ERNST WEISS	*Franziska*
	Jarmila
EDITH WHARTON	*Glimpses of the Moon*
FLORIAN ZELLER	*Artificial Snow*
	Julien Parme
	Lovers or Something Like It
	The Fascination of Evil
STEFAN ZWEIG	*Amok and Other Stories*
	Beware of Pity
	Burning Secret
	Casanova: A Study in Self-Portraiture
	A Chess Story
	The Collected Stories of Stefan Zweig
	Confusion
	Fear
	The Governess and Other Stories
	Journey into the Past
	Letter from an Unknown Woman and Other Stories
	Magellan
	Marie Antoinette
	Mary Stuart
	Mental Healers: Mesmer, Eddy, Freud
	Selected Stories
	Shooting Stars: Ten Historical Miniatures
	The Struggle with the Daemon: Hölderlin, Kleist, Nietzsche
	Twilight and Moonbeam Alley
	The World of Yesterday
	Wondrak and Other Stories